INSIDE the MUSEUM

A Children's Guide to
THE METROPOLITAN MUSEUM OF ART

Joy Richardson

THE METROPOLITAN MUSEUM OF ART

Publication of this book has been made possible in part by the Horace W. Goldsmith Foundation.

I am grateful to the staff members of every Museum department who have generously contributed their time, ideas, enthusiasm, and expert knowledge in the course of this book's creation. The Education Department has been especially helpful in arranging visits, answering questions, and reviewing my manuscript. My thanks also to the staff of the Department of Special Publications, particularly Robie Rogge, Publishing Manager; Carolyn Vaughan, Editor; Katherine van Kessel, Production Manager; Rachel Mustalish, Editorial Assistant; and Emily Eisenberg, Senior Product Developer. I am indebted to them, and to Marleen Adlerbaum, the book's designer, for their skill and tenacity in guiding the book through each stage of its development.

JR

Thanks to Kevin Avery, Thomas Bagby, Zainab Bahrani, Carrie Rebora Barratt, Luca Bigini, Lucia Bigini, Paula Bigini, Malcolm Daniel, Othman El-Jitan, Chris Giftos, Clifford Hayes, Laurence Kanter, Dan Kershaw, Zachary Lewis, Laurence Libin, Herb Martinez, Lisa Moore, Aidan O'Connor, Faon O'Connor, Chris Paulocik, Carlos Picón, Stewart S. Pollens, Lowery Sims, Charles Tantillo, Carmela Vollaro, the Wantagh Middle School, and Elizabeth Wyckoff.

Published in 1993 by The Metropolitan Museum of Art, New York
Reissued 1999, 2010
Copyright © 1993 by The Metropolitan Museum of Art

Printed in China

19 18 17 16 15 14 13 12 11 10   13 12 11 10 9

Produced by the Department of Special Publications, The Metropolitan Museum of Art

Book designed by Marleen Adlerbaum

Cover illustration by John Kerschbaum, 2008 © John Kerschbaum. Illustration made possible by The Aronson Family Foundation.

Grateful acknowledgment is made for permission to reprint the following copyrighted material: "The Great Figure" by William Carlos Williams, from *The Collected Poems of William Carlos Williams, 1909–1939, vol. I.* Copyright 1938 by New Directions Publishing Corporation. Reprinted by permission of New Directions Publishing Corporation and Carcanet Press Limited.

Illustrations on pages 5, 13, 15, 17, 18, 23, 25, 27, 33, 36–37, 45, 47, 62, and 65 by Teresa Anderko
Diagrams on pages 16, 20, 22, and 37 by Barry Girsh

Library of Congress Catalog Card Number: 93-77292
ISBN 978-0-87099-666-5

The Metropolitan Museum of Art
1000 Fifth Avenue
New York, NY 10028
212.570.3894
www.metmuseum.org

7441

THE METROPOLITAN MUSEUM OF ART is a magic show of mystery and magnificence. Here you can travel the planet and slip back through time, as works of art conjure up their creators and the worlds in which they lived.

This book will introduce you to a sample of the Museum's treasures. It will also take you behind the scenes to find out how the Museum works.

You can use this book in the Museum or at home, finding stories to surprise you, facts to amuse you, questions to puzzle you, and activities to entertain you.

A Growing Museum

The Metropolitan Museum of Art was founded in 1870. The Museum held exhibitions in two temporary homes until the City of New York provided a large area in Central Park with plenty of room for a new building. The first wing of the Museum's permanent home was opened in 1880.

The Museum steadily grew larger and grander. At the beginning of this century, a statelynew wing was built facing Fifth Avenue, with the spacious Great Hall and Grand Staircase behind it. New galleries have been constructed to house the Museum's many collections.

The building is now twenty times bigger than it was in 1880, and it has filled all the space originally provided by the city.

The front of the Museum today

EYE SPY
Can you see the differences between the architects' plan for the front of the Museum (below) and the way it looks now (above)?

The architects' plan for the front of the Museum, 1890s

The stone blocks above the columns were never finished. The carvings would have been too expensive.

The steps to the front entrance were changed in 1970, because they were too narrow.

Today the front steps are a favorite meeting place for New Yorkers and tourists.

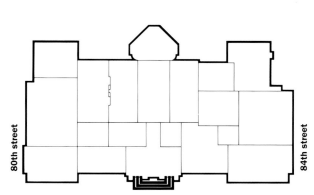

From end to end the Museum is as long as four New York City blocks.

80th street

84th street

FASCINATING FACT
The Metropolitan Museum of Art is one of the largest art museums in the world. The building is a quarter of a mile long and its area is more than 1.4 million square feet.

In 1908, about 800,000 people visited the Museum.

Now, about 4.5 million people visit the Museum each year. If they all held hands, the line would stretch from the Museum to the Pacific Ocean.

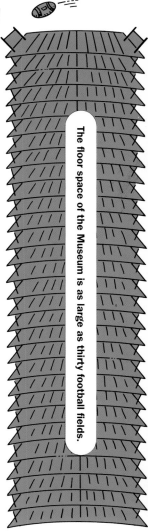

The floor space of the Museum is as large as thirty football fields.

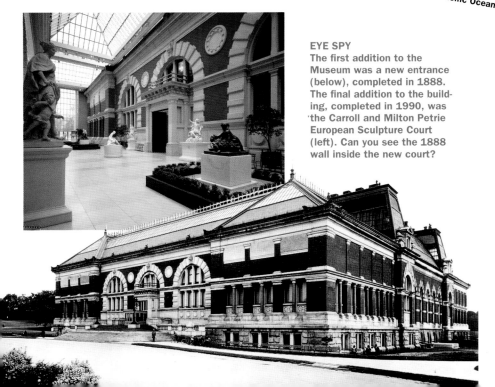

EYE SPY
The first addition to the Museum was a new entrance (below), completed in 1888. The final addition to the building, completed in 1990, was the Carroll and Milton Petrie European Sculpture Court (left). Can you see the 1888 wall inside the new court?

On the Way In

Every visitor to the Museum receives a colored button. Millions of these buttons have now been made, in more than a hundred different colors, and they have been taken home to every part of the world.

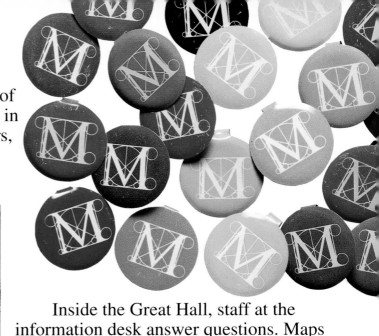

The Great Hall, with the information desk

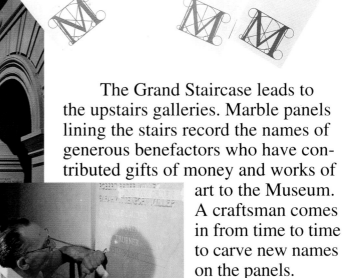

Inside the Great Hall, staff at the information desk answer questions. Maps of the Museum are available in seven different languages. What are they? (Answer on page 72.)

The Grand Staircase leads to the upstairs galleries. Marble panels lining the stairs record the names of generous benefactors who have contributed gifts of money and works of art to the Museum. A craftsman comes in from time to time to carve new names on the panels.

The Grand Staircase

The Museum in Bloom

Fresh flowers are always blooming in the Great Hall. They are picked, packed, and flown in from Holland each weekend, then arranged on Monday while the Museum is closed.

There are gardens and plants throughout the Museum. Gardeners water them and take care of them.

Keeping Watch

Guards in blue uniforms keep an eye on every section of the Museum. They watch to make sure no damage is done to works of art, and they help visitors find their way around the galleries.

When the Museum closes, the guards shepherd visitors out and check to see that no one is left behind. Watchmen patrol the building throughout the night.

Through the Keyhole

You can walk for miles through the galleries in the Museum and never run out of things to see. Yet most of the Museum's work goes on behind closed doors. You would probably never guess that it takes a staff of 2,500 to keep the Museum running! Here is your chance to peep through the keyhole and find out what goes on behind the scenes.

Cleaning Up

As soon as the Museum closes in the evening, cleaners get to work with mops and brooms and buffing machines. The cleaning goes on all night. Special cleaning jobs wait until Monday when the Museum is closed for the day.

Technicians take care of sculptures and furniture and dust them gently.

Mopping the floors

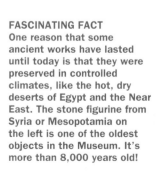

Dusting a vase
Vase. French, 19th century. Malachite, height 67½ in., 1819.

EYE SPY
Can you spot the sensors in this gallery?

Controlling the Climate

Changes from hot to cold or damp to dry can damage works of art, so it is important to control the climate inside the building.

Around the Museum there are 1,600 small sensors that measure temperature and the amount of moisture in the air. Nine miles of wiring link them all to a central computer, which operates day and night. If the air heats up or dries out, adjustments are quickly made.

Seated Female Figurine. Northern Syria or Mesopotamia, 7th–6th millennium B.C. Stone, height 1⁹⁄₁₆ in.

FASCINATING FACT
One reason that some ancient works have lasted until today is that they were preserved in controlled climates, like the hot, dry deserts of Egypt and the Near East. The stone figurine from Syria or Mesopotamia on the left is one of the oldest objects in the Museum. It's more than 8,000 years old!

The climate control computer room

Craftspeople at Work

There are fourteen workshops behind the scenes where craftspeople use their skills to keep the whole building in good working condition.

Plumbers mend pipes, lampers fit light bulbs, and roofers keep the Museum watertight. Other shops are equipped for working with wood, metal, stone, paint, and Plexiglas. There are even locksmiths, elevator repairmen, and electricians.

The carpentry shop

On the Move

When exhibitions change or new works come to the Museum, works of art have to be moved around. Most of this work goes on when the galleries are closed, to avoid bumping into visitors.

The Museum's movers pack and unpack works of art, and move art in and out of and around the Museum. They handle everything very carefully.

The movers figure out the best way to move things. Sometimes this can be quite a challenge!

Movers carefully lift a painting from its crate.

Movers lower a large sculpture still in its crate into place.

The sculpture *Water Stone* by Isamu Noguchi is made of solid stone and weighs 2,600 pounds. The sculptor supervised as it was lowered into place with a pulley.

Large sculptures are carefully padded while they are moved. This one was lowered into place.

Keeping Records

With more than two million works of art, the Museum has to keep good records of everything in its collections.

As soon as a new object comes to the Museum, it is given an identification number, called an accession number.

FASCINATING FACT
The very first work of art to enter the Museum's collections was this Roman coffin, or sarcophagus. Its accession number is 70.1, because it was the first object acquired in 1870.

Garland Sarcophagus
Marble
Roman, Severan period, ca. A.D. 200–225
Found at Tarsus, in southern Turkey, in 1863
This was the first gift accepted by the Museum.

The back and cover of the sarcophagus are unfinished and its inscription tablet is blank, which may imply that it went unsold in antiquity. Garlands of oak leaves, supported by two Erotes and four Victories, adorn the front and sides. Medusa heads fill the spaces above the garlands, except in the center of the sarcophagus front, where there is the blank inscription tablet. Six Erotes hunt various wild animals along the front face of the cover, while two others stand at the corners. On the left end, Eros awakens Psyche with an arrow, and on the right, they embrace.

Gift of Abdo Debbas, 1870
70.1

You can find information about each work of art, including its accession number, on the label next to it in the gallery.

Garland Sarcophagus. Roman, about A.D. 200–225. Marble; length 87½, height 52½ in.

New works of art are photographed in a studio high above the dome of the Great Hall. Many different kinds of cameras and lenses are used.

The history of and important facts about each object are kept on index cards in the catalogue department. There are more than 1,600 drawers full of these index cards.

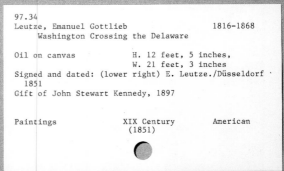

```
97.34
Leutze, Emanuel Gottlieb                          1816-1868
       Washington Crossing the Delaware

Oil on canvas                      H. 12 feet, 5 inches,
                                   W. 21 feet, 3 inches
Signed and dated: (lower right) E. Leutze./Düsseldorf
   1851
Gift of John Stewart Kennedy, 1897


Paintings              XIX Century            American
                        (1851)
```

EYE SPY
Can you find the accession number on this card?
(Answer on page 72.)

Stored Away

More than half of the works of art in the Museum are stored away behind the scenes. Some are too fragile to remain on display for long periods of time. Some are being studied by scholars. And some are stored because there isn't room for everything in the galleries. Works in storage are carefully looked after until it's their turn to be put on view.

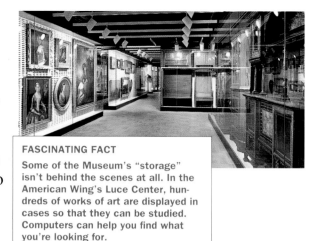

FASCINATING FACT

Some of the Museum's "storage" isn't behind the scenes at all. In the American Wing's Luce Center, hundreds of works of art are displayed in cases so that they can be studied. Computers can help you find what you're looking for.

Textile conservators work on a 15th-century tapestry.

Conservation

Like people, works of art grow old and fragile. Heat, light, fingerprints, movement, and even the sound of voices can damage them.

Conservators are experts in the different materials and techniques that are used to make works of art. They use this knowledge to treat the works and to preserve the Museum's collections for the future.

Conservators use scientific equipment for investigations. They also use their hands, skillfully and patiently, to clean and repair works of art that can never be replaced.

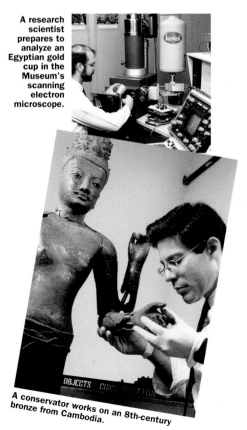

A research scientist prepares to analyze an Egyptian gold cup in the Museum's scanning electron microscope.

A conservator removes modern upholstery from an 18th-century German settee. An X-ray shows the original structure underneath.

There are separate conservation centers in the Museum for paintings, works on paper, objects, textiles, armor, musical instruments, and books.

A conservator works on an 8th-century bronze from Cambodia.

2. Making plans

3. At the drawing board

4. The exhibition in miniature

1. Choosing works of art

Getting Ready for an Exhibition

In addition to displaying objects from its many collections, the Museum also organizes special, temporary exhibitions. The exhibitions can be about a particular artist or about a style or period of art. Works are borrowed from other museums and from people all over the world. It can take several years to plan an exhibition and weeks to get the galleries ready.

Curators decide what will be in the exhibition and how the works will be displayed. They write a catalogue, or book, and wall labels to tell about the art. Designers draw plans and make detailed scale models to show where things will go. They even put tiny copies of works of art in the models. Then the galleries are prepared and the works of art are installed. Banners on the front of the building tell people what's going on.

When a new permanent gallery is opened, or an old one is rearranged, the same procedures take place, except that works are all from the Museum's own collections.

EYE SPY
Which photograph is the designer's scale model and which is the actual gallery?
(Answer on page 72.)

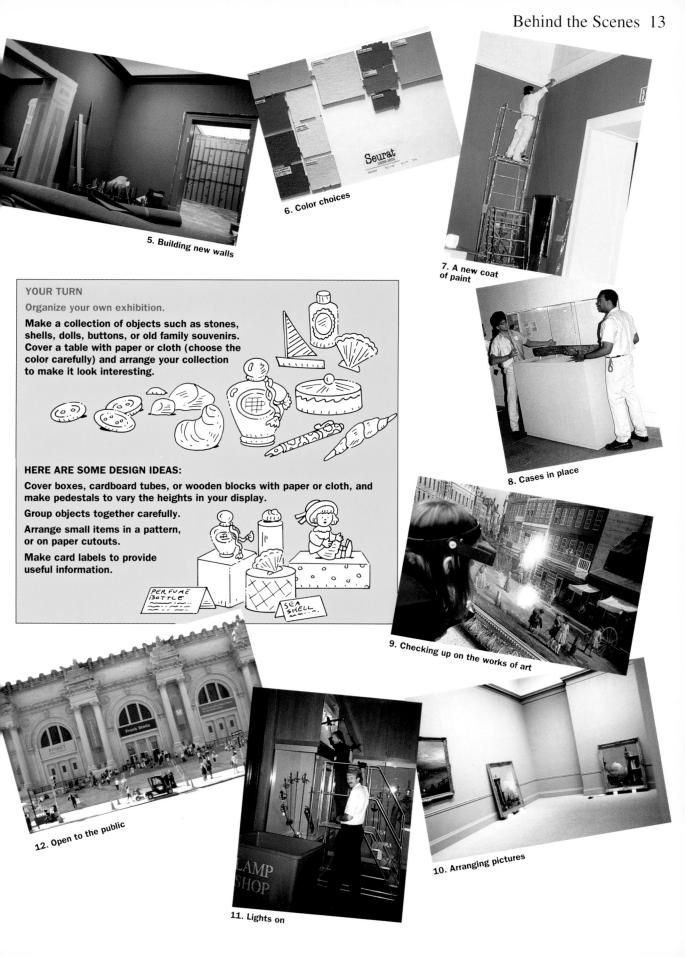

5. Building new walls

6. Color choices

7. A new coat of paint

8. Cases in place

9. Checking up on the works of art

YOUR TURN

Organize your own exhibition.

Make a collection of objects such as stones, shells, dolls, buttons, or old family souvenirs. Cover a table with paper or cloth (choose the color carefully) and arrange your collection to make it look interesting.

HERE ARE SOME DESIGN IDEAS:

Cover boxes, cardboard tubes, or wooden blocks with paper or cloth, and make pedestals to vary the heights in your display.

Group objects together carefully.

Arrange small items in a pattern, or on paper cutouts.

Make card labels to provide useful information.

PERFUME BOTTLE

SEA SHELL

12. Open to the public

11. Lights on

10. Arranging pictures

Discussing a painting in the storeroom

Curators

"Curator" really means one who cares for. Curators are in charge of the works of art in the Museum. They decide what should be displayed in each gallery, and they arrange the displays to help people understand and appreciate the art. Curators find new works to add to the Museum's collections, and they organize special exhibitions.

Curators also study the works of art in order to learn more about them. They piece together information by looking carefully at the works themselves, by studying scientific investigations, by reading books and articles, and by talking with other experts around the world.

Researching works of art

Examining sculpture in the gallery

In the Museum there are eighteen curatorial departments. Every work of art in the Museum belongs in one of these departments. Each department has its own curators and an area of the Museum where its collections are on view.

What's Inside

Different kinds of museums have different kinds of collections. Some art museums collect only paintings, drawings, and sculpture. The Metropolitan Museum also has some more unusual collections, such as musical instruments, costumes, and arms and armor. Everything you see at the Museum was chosen because of its beauty and artistry, whether it was made to be looked at or for use in everyday life. All the works in the Museum were made with human skill—there are no dinosaurs! (They are across Central Park at the American Museum of Natural History.)

This book takes you through each curatorial collection, inviting you to enjoy some of the Museum's treasures.

Turban Helmet. Iranian, 1450–1500. Steel and silver, height 13³/₈ in.

Violin. Antonio Stradivari, Italian, 1644–1737. Curly maple, spruce, and other materials; length 23⁵/₈ in.; 1691.

FASCINATING FACT
There are more than two million objects in the Museum's collections. If you spent a minute looking at each one, you would have to come to the Museum every day for more than thirteen years to see them all!

IN THE EGYPTIAN COLLECTION you'll find statues and temples, models and mummy cases, gleaming gold and bright blue objects. Many of the works were discovered during archaeological excavations, or "digs," sponsored by the Museum.

A Case for a Mummy

In ancient Egypt people believed that the dead went on a journey to a new world, where daily activities continued much as they had in the realm of the living. The soul of the dead person still needed somewhere to live, so a lot of work went into preserving the body. It was dried and wrapped with many layers of cloth to make a mummy.

The wooden coffin on the left, now empty, was made 3,000 years ago to contain the mummy of a temple attendant named Henettawy. It was decorated with magic signs and spells to protect Henettawy's soul as it traveled through the underworld.

EYE SPY
Can you find these magic signs?

the sky goddess spreading her wings in protection

magic eyes, powerful symbols of protection

the jackal-headed god in charge of preparing the body

the scarab beetle pushing the morning sun over the horizon

From the Nile to New York

For 2,000 years the Temple of Dendur stood beside the River Nile in Egypt. When a dam was planned that would permanently raise the water level above Dendur and other ancient temples, the buildings were taken apart and moved to save them from drowning. The Egyptian Government offered Dendur to the United States in thanks for American help in the rescue effort. Arrangements were made in 1968 to bring the temple to the Metropolitan Museum, where a new wing to house the temple opened ten years later.

Outer Coffin of Henettawy. Egyptian (Thebes, Deir el-Bahri), about 1000 B.C. Gessoed and painted wood, length 79⅞ in.

1. The temple in Egypt

2. Egyptian stonemasons took the temple apart stone by stone, numbering each stone so the building could be perfectly rebuilt. The stones were stored on an island in Egypt.

3. The blocks were shipped to New York.

4. A bubble tent was installed next to the Museum to store the blocks.

5. Work began on a new wing to house the temple.

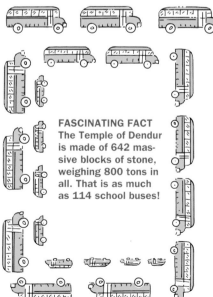

6. The temple was reconstructed inside the new wing. Each enormous block was gently hoisted into position.

Inside its giant showcase the Temple of Dendur is bathed in light and overlooks a pool of water. You can almost imagine you are seeing it across the waters of the Nile.

Temple of Dendur. Egyptian, about 15 B.C. Sandstone, length of gateway and temple, 82 ft.

FASCINATING FACT
The Temple of Dendur is made of 642 massive blocks of stone, weighing 800 tons in all. That is as much as 114 school buses!

Magic Models

Mekutra was a king's chancellor in ancient Egypt. In 1920, archaeologists from the Metropolitan Museum were excavating his tomb but finding nothing. Tomb robbers had been there before them.

Late one day, a workman noticed a crack where the wall of the tomb met the floor. Expecting to find another empty hole, the expedition leader shone a flashlight through the gap. What he saw left him in a daze of excitement.

"The beam of light shot into a world of four thousand years ago, and I was gazing down into the midst of a myriad of brightly painted little men going this way and that."

The secret chamber was packed with twenty-three models of Mekutra's everyday life.

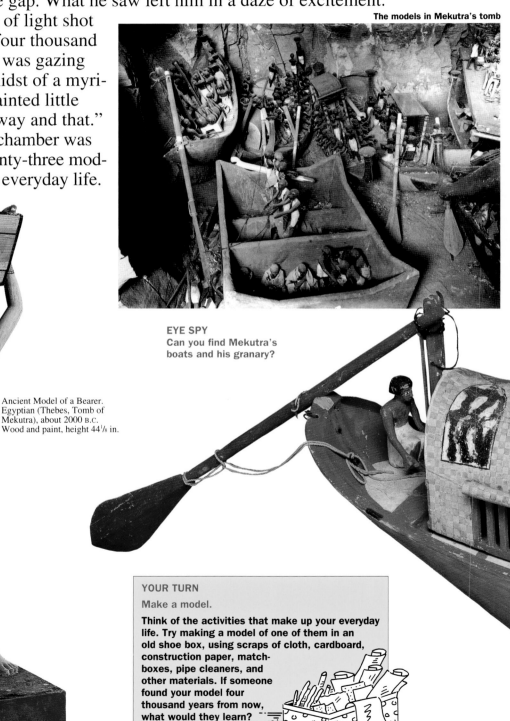

The models in Mekutra's tomb

EYE SPY
Can you find Mekutra's boats and his granary?

Ancient Model of a Bearer.
Egyptian (Thebes, Tomb of Mekutra), about 2000 B.C.
Wood and paint, height 44 1/8 in.

YOUR TURN

Make a model.

Think of the activities that make up your everyday life. Try making a model of one of them in an old shoe box, using scraps of cloth, cardboard, construction paper, matchboxes, pipe cleaners, and other materials. If someone found your model four thousand years from now, what would they learn?

Mekutra was a rich nobleman. He had servants to farm his fields, look after his cattle, prepare his food, weave his cloth, and sail his boats. He wanted this pleasant life to continue forever, so he had models made of all these activities. The models were buried with him when he died. He believed that the models would magically come to life so his servants could carry on their work and take care of his spirit.

Ancient Model of a Granary. Egyptian (Thebes, Tomb of Mekutra), about 2000 B.C. Wood and paint, length 29⅛ in., width 22⅞ in.

Baskets of grain are being brought into Mekutra's granary, and scribes are keeping count on papyrus rolls and wooden tablets. Men with buckets measure the grain before it is poured into storage bins. There is still grain on the floor that was put in by the ancient model makers 4,000 years ago!

Mekutra's traveling boat is out on the River Nile. Servants row the boat while Mekutra sits comfortably, smelling a lotus and listening to a harpist and a singer. The singer holds his hand in front of his face to produce a warbling sound.

Ancient Model of a Traveling Boat. Egyptian (Thebes, Tomb of Mekutra), about 2000 B.C. Wood and paint, length 56 in.

Princess's Jewelry

This magnificent necklace was made almost 4,000 years ago, from gold and colored stones. It was worn by a king's daughter, and when she died, it was buried with her in her grave near the pyramid of Senwosret II, king of Egypt.

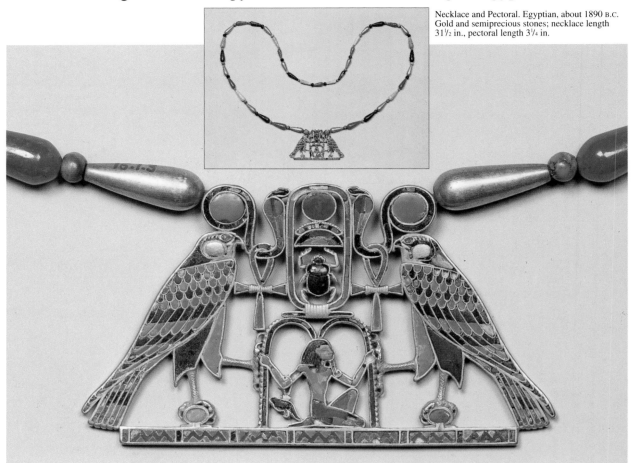

Necklace and Pectoral. Egyptian, about 1890 B.C. Gold and semiprecious stones; necklace length 31½ in., pectoral length 3¼ in.

The pectoral hangs from the necklace like a charm. It is made up of hieroglyphic signs, all of which have meanings. It asks the sun god to grant long life to Senwosret II.

EYE SPY
The pectoral is just 3¼ inches across. Can you guess how many pieces of colored stone it contains? (Answer on page 72.)

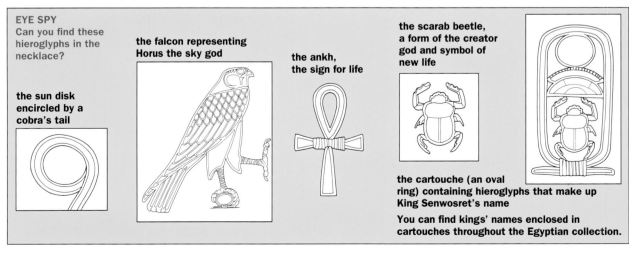

EYE SPY
Can you find these hieroglyphs in the necklace?

the sun disk encircled by a cobra's tail

the falcon representing Horus the sky god

the ankh, the sign for life

the scarab beetle, a form of the creator god and symbol of new life

the cartouche (an oval ring) containing hieroglyphs that make up King Senwosret's name

You can find kings' names enclosed in cartouches throughout the Egyptian collection.

BEHIND THE SCENES
Why is Nephthys's golden face red? Object conservators used a powerful microscope and other scientific tests to study the coffin face. They discovered that the red color is not original. It is a natural tarnish that can develop over thousands of years when gold contains some silver.

Coffin of Nephthys (detail). Egyptian (Meir), about 1850 B.C. Cartonnage, gold leaf, paint, and inlaid stones; coffin length 70²/₃ in.

Hippopotamus on Guard

This little hippopotamus is decorated with lotus flowers that grew in the marshes where hippopotami roamed. It was placed in a tomb to ward off dangerous forces of nature.

The hippo is made of faience, a mixture of ground quartz, natural salts, and water, which was modeled, dried, and then fired. When the figure was heated, the surface became glassy, and copper in the mixture made the hippo bright blue, a favorite Egyptian color.

FASCINATING FACT
This hippo is especially popular at the Museum. It has even been nicknamed "William."

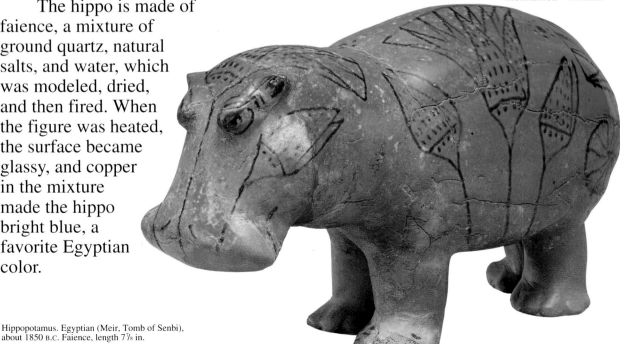

Hippopotamus. Egyptian (Meir, Tomb of Senbi), about 1850 B.C. Faience, length 7⁷/₈ in.

THE MUSEUM'S COLLECTION OF ART OF THE ANCIENT NEAR EAST spans a period of almost 8,000 years, from about 7,000 B.C. to A.D. 651, and an area from Turkey to Pakistan. These ancient civilizations were quite advanced: They built cities, forts, and palaces, and they developed a system of writing.

King Ashurnasirpal's Palace

In the ninth century B.C., King Ashurnasirpal II ruled over Assyria (now northern Iraq). He fought wars and hunted lions and built himself a splendid new palace at Nimrud. Colossal sculptures of winged beasts with human heads guarded the doorways to keep out evil spirits.

Written in Stone

Inscriptions were cut into the palace walls to record the king's titles and his glorious deeds. Again and again stonemasons chiseled the message

Human-headed Winged Lion. Assyrian, about 883–859 B.C. Limestone, height 10 ft. 2½ in.

Ashurnasirpal II   **The Mighty King**

EYE SPY
Can you see the winged lion's five legs? From the front it seems that the lion is solidly standing guard, while from the side he is on the prowl.

This ancient writing is called cuneiform, meaning "wedge shaped." It is the earliest form of writing, invented about 5,000 years ago.

The triangular marks could be chiseled into stone or pressed onto clay tablets with a stylus, a writing instrument made from a reed or a bone.

Relief of a Winged Deity, from Ashurnasirpal's palace. Assyrian, about 883–859 B.C. Alabaster, 94 × 66½ in. The cuneiform inscription runs across the middle.

Tribute Bearer

The Assyrian kings conquered the lands around them. They grew wealthy from captured treasure and from tribute paid by their subjects.

The figurine on the right shows a man bringing tribute: an oryx (a kind of antelope), a monkey, and a fine spotted leopard skin. It was probably made by Phoenicians, neighbors of the Assyrians, and it is carved of precious ivory, which came from elephant tusks. Originally, it decorated a piece of furniture and was covered in gold leaf and inlaid with colored stones and other materials.

After 200 years, the palace at Nimrud was destroyed by a conquering army. The invaders did not think much of the ivory objects collected by the Assyrian kings. They stripped off the gold and decoration and then threw the ivories away.

Nubian Tribute Bearer. Assyrian, Phoenician style, 8th century B.C. Ivory, height 5¹⁵/₁₆ in.

More than 2,500 years later the palace was excavated. The little tribute bearer was dug out of the ground to be enjoyed once more.

Austen Henry Layard, plate 2 from *Monuments of Nineveh I.* Published in London by John Murray, 1849.

The stone sculptures in Ashurnasirpal's palace were painted. An archaeologist who excavated the palace drew this picture to show how it may have looked.

YOUR TURN

Try some cuneiform writing.

1. Cut a strip of light cardboard 3/4 inch wide and 2 inches long. (This size will make a stylus that is most like those that ancient peoples used. You can make it bigger if you want to.)

2. Draw lines 1/4 inch from each long side to divide the strip into thirds, then cut off two of the corners, following the diagram.

3. Fold the card along the lines to make a hollow triangle, then stick tape down the side and over the angled end.

4. Use your stylus to make cuneiform marks on a tablet of soft modeling clay. Try writing Ashurnasirpal's title, or make up your own secret code.

THE DEPARTMENT OF ASIAN ART includes the arts of China, Japan, Korea, India, and Southeast Asia, with works from about 2,000 B.C. to our own century.

Scrolls and Seals

The ancient Chinese handscroll above shows a man watching geese on the water. The scroll is about three feet long: If you had been invited to look at it, you would have sat down quietly and unrolled it bit by bit, feasting your eyes on each part as it came into view.

The red stamps are seal marks. They have been added to the scroll over the centuries by different owners and by people who have enjoyed looking at it.

Chinese artists and collectors all had their own seals. The designs were planned on paper and then carved onto polished stone with a knife.

Seal Paste Box, Tortoise Seal, and Bamboo Seal. Chinese. Box: Porcelain, height 1½ in., 1662–1722. Tortoise Seal: Seal of Chou-Shun-Ch'ang (1584–1626), silver, height ¹⁵/₁₆ in., 1600–25. Bamboo Seal: Bamboo, 19th century, height 3 in.

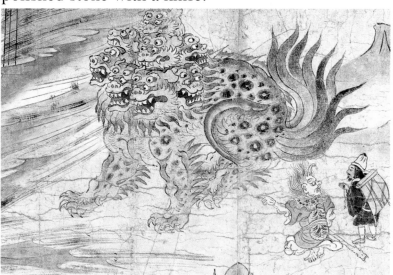

If you unroll one thirteenth-century Japanese scroll, you'll find this monstrous beast guarding the gates of the underworld.

EYE SPY
Can you count the dragon's heads?
(Answer on page 72.)

Tenjin Engi. Japanese, 13th century. Detail from a handscroll, ink and color on paper; 12¼ in. x 18 ft. 5⅞ in.

Wang Hsi-chih Watching Geese. Ch'ien Hsüan, Chinese, about 1235–1300. Handscroll, ink, colors, and gold on paper; 9½ x 36 in.

YOUR TURN

Make your own seal.

1. Cut a potato in half and cut away the sides to make a square end.

2. Plan a simple design on paper. If you use your initials, be sure to reverse the letters so that they print the right way.

3. Transfer your design to the potato by cutting away lines with the point of a pencil.

4. Put a thin sponge or some paper towels on a plate to make a printing pad. Dampen the pad slightly and add some liquid paint, such as poster paint. Turn the pad over and press your seal into it until the color comes through. Print your seal on paper.

Shiva Nataraja, Lord of the Dance. Indian, late 12th-early 13th centuries. Bronze, height 25¾ in.

Lord of the Dance

Shiva Nataraja, Lord of the Dance, is a Hindu god. Hindus believe that he dances on and on to keep the universe circling around from death and destruction to birth and new life.

This bronze statue was made in India about 800 years ago. It has a hole at the bottom so it could be placed on a pole and carried in a procession.

The statue is still, but it looks as if it's about to move.

EYE SPY

Can you find these parts of the statue?

- the flaming universe circling around Shiva
- Shiva's long flowing hair
- double arms moving in rhythm with the dance
- a drum in one hand tapping out the beat
- the demon Ignorance being trampled underfoot

A Chinese Garden

The Astor Court was built at the Museum by Chinese workmen with materials specially brought from China.

The garden is a peaceful place where you can let your eyes wander and your imagination take flight. It looks plain and simple, but every detail is designed for a special effect.

Rocks are important in Chinese gardens. They are miniature mountains, bringing magnificent landscapes to mind. These fantastic rocks with their knobbly bumps and see-through holes become soaring peaks towering above rocky foothills. Seen from different angles they may also turn into strange beings and magical creatures.

Water makes a gentle contrast, trickling down a waterfall into the fishpond in the corner.

EYE SPY

The Chinese garden represents opposites that go together in nature. Can you complete the pairs and find both parts in the garden? (The first one is done for you.)

- hard...soft
- dark...
- rough...
- dry...
- closed...
- straight...

(Answers on page 72.)

The Astor Court, completed in 1981

The garden is made so that you can look at it in a thousand ways without ever getting bored. The lattice shapes in the walls cast different patterns of light and shadow to keep your eyes interested. As you look around, the view keeps changing, framed by doorways, rooflines, walls, and pillars.

YOUR TURN

Make some viewing frames.

1. Cut some three-inch squares from cardboard or paper.

2. In the center of each one cut out a small shape— a circle, a rectangle, a slit—to make a frame.

3. Look through the frames to make your own views of the garden.

You can use your frames in the Museum, at home, outside, or with this guide. They can help you to see things differently and to look at them more closely.

ISLAMIC ART is inspired by the religion of Islam, founded by Muhammad in 622. Over the years Islam spread from Arabia across Asia and into Africa and Europe, influencing the cultures of many countries.

Patterns Everywhere

Islamic artists are masters of pattern. They make beautiful, intricate patterns to decorate every surface. Islamic patterns are usually made up of geometric shapes or from flowers and leaves with intertwining stems.

Carved wooden doors inlaid with ivory
Pair of Doors. Egyptian, probably second half of the 14th century. Wood and ivory, 65 × 30¹/₂ in.

These wooden doors are made up of a repeating geometric pattern of twelve-sided figures, called dodecagons, enclosing twelve-pointed stars.

A niche made of mosaic pieces of colored tile
Prayer Niche. Iranian, about 1354. Ceramic, 11 ft. 3 in. × 7 ft. 6 in.

A wall panel of painted tiles
Tiles. Syrian, second half of
the 16th century. Ceramic,
33 x 22 in.

YOUR TURN
Make a pattern. The mosaic niche, the wooden doors, the
painted tiles, and the woolen carpet are all made up of
interlocking parts. Try drawing one small section of one of
the patterns. Can you figure out what shapes it contains
and how they fit together to make a repeating pattern?

A carpet of knotted wool
Rug. Turkish, 19th century. Wool, 50 ¼ x 71 in.

Prince Riding an Elephant. Attributed to Khem Karan. Indian, late 16th-early 17th centuries. Ink, colors,
and gold on paper, 12¼ x 18½ in.

Elephant Ride

Islamic artists recorded in pictures the stories of
heroic achievements and events from everyday life.
Here a prince is riding an elephant, while servants
swish away troublesome insects with fly whisks.

The painting is full of life—it is not hard to imagine
the bells jingling furiously as the elephant's feet pound the ground.

The picture was painted in about 1600 in India, during the reign of the
emperor Akbar.

BEHIND THE SCENES
When the Museum bought
Prince Riding an Elephant,
it was rather dirty and had
a red line running across it.
Conservators cleaned the
surface very gently. They
removed the red line by
cutting it away with a fine
scalpel blade while looking
through a microscope—
just like surgeons—as this
conservator is doing.

Light fades colors and
makes paper fragile, so
paintings like this are kept
away from bright light and
displays are changed often.

THE DEPARTMENT OF GREEK AND ROMAN ART has acquired a great number of ancient works of art since 1870, when that Roman sarcophagus became the first object to belong to the Museum (see page 10). The collections include Greek vases, Cypriot statues, Roman wall paintings, and objects made of glass and of silver.

Panathenaic Prize Amphora. Nikias. Greek, about 560–555 B.C. Terracotta, height 24⅝ in. Below: detail.

First Prize: The Original Olympics

In about 550 B.C., the winner of a 200-yard running race received this vase, or amphora, filled with olive oil as his prize.

Sports competitions were very popular in ancient Greece. Our modern Olympic games are based on competitions like the great Panathenaic Games, held every four years in Athens. Instead of receiving medals, winners at the Panathenaic Games were rewarded with vases like this one.

One side, labeled "men's foot race," shows runners in action. The goddess Athena, patroness of Athens and of the games, appears on the other side.

EYE SPY
Can you see the signature of the potter Nikias?

By the sixth century B.C., Athenian pottery was among the finest in the world. This elegant vase would have been treasured and admired long after the oil ran out.

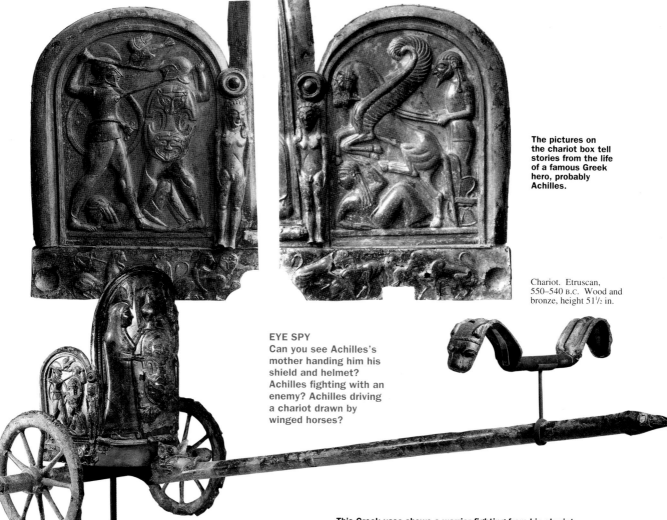

The pictures on the chariot box tell stories from the life of a famous Greek hero, probably Achilles.

Chariot. Etruscan, 550–540 B.C. Wood and bronze, height 51½ in.

EYE SPY
Can you see Achilles's mother handing him his shield and helmet? Achilles fighting with an enemy? Achilles driving a chariot drawn by winged horses?

Chariot Race

Horse-drawn chariots like this one once carried noble warriors into battle. The warrior stood in the chariot box, armed with spear and shield, while his driver urged on the horses as they thundered into the fray.

This finely decorated chariot was never battered in a fight. It was made in the sixth century B.C. to be buried in the tomb of an Etruscan warrior. The Etruscans ruled much of Italy before the rise of the Roman Empire. Influenced by Greek art, they produced fine sculpture and metalwork.

This Greek vase shows a warrior fighting from his chariot.

Detail from an Amphora. Greek, about 540 B.C. Terracotta, height 15⅛ in.

As the centuries passed, the chariot fell to pieces in the tomb, and the wooden pole rotted away. The bronze fragments have been fitted together again and attached to a new pole.

THE WORKS IN THE DEPARTMENT OF MEDIEVAL ART were created in Europe during the period we call the "Middle Ages." This was the period in Western civilization between the birth of Jesus Christ and the time of Christopher Columbus. It was the age of knights and ladies, castles and cathedrals.

A Metal Foot

What in the world was this used for? It was made about A.D. 400 from a mixture of metals. Copper in the mixture has turned green with age.

The sandaled foot, modeled in detail right down to its toenails, was used as a lamp. Lamp oil fed a rope wick that sat in the spout next to the big toe. The lamp hung from a chain, spreading its light wide.

Hanging Lamp,
in the shape of a foot.
Byzantine, 4th–5th centuries.
Copper alloy, height 5 1/16 in., length 6 1/2 in.

Playing Games

Games such as backgammon, checkers, and chess were all popular in the Middle Ages. These game pieces from Europe were made more than 800 years ago. Carved from the ivory tusks of walruses, they were left creamy white or stained dark red.

The game pieces may have been kept in a container like this one. This box was made of wood, covered with a thin layer of plaster and painted.

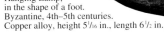

Game Piece, showing Hercules throwing King Diomedes to his man-eating horses. German, 1140–50. Walrus ivory, diameter 2 3/4 in.

Game Piece, showing Samson slaying the Philistines with the jawbone of an ass. German, 1140–50. Walrus ivory, diameter 2 3/4 in.

Box. German,
late 13th century.
Painted wood, length 10 3/16 in.

EYE SPY
The painter played a game with the animal heads along the top of the box. Can you spot the trick? (Answer on page 72.)

HINT: Try looking at the box upside down!

A Story in Glass

Stained-glass windows told stories. This window from a church in Germany was made 500 years ago. As sunlight shone through, the glowing glass told the Christmas story.

It took great skill to make a panel of stained glass like this. We know how it was done because a medieval monk wrote down instructions in a book.

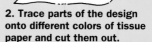

This artisan is joining pieces of glass together with lead.

The Glazier. Jost Amman, Swiss, 1539–1591. Woodcut, 1568.

The Monk's Instructions

1. Melt ash and sand in metal pots. Add metallic oxides and ground-up old glass to make different colors.

2. Collect some glass on the end of a pipe and blow to make a long balloon.

3. Slit the balloon down the side and flatten it into a sheet.

4. Draw a picture on a wooden board. Put colored glass on top and trace the outlines of the figures in the scene.

5. Cut out the pieces of glass by cracking the glass with a red-hot iron and trimming it with a special cutting tool.

6. Paint lines and shading with a dark pigment.

7. Make lead casings in a mold and bend them around each piece of glass to hold it tight against its neighbor. Solder the joints with tin and lead mixed together.

8. Surround each scene with an iron frame and assemble the window panel by panel.

The Nativity. German, from the Carmelite church, Boppard on the Rhine, 1440–46. Stained glass, 41½ x 28½ in.

YOUR TURN

Make your own "stained glass."

1. Draw a simple design on paper. Large shapes with straight edges work best.

2. Trace parts of the design onto different colors of tissue paper and cut them out.

3. Cut strips of kitchen foil about 1/2 inch to 1 inch wide to make "lead."

4. Join the "glass" pieces together with "lead." Tape each piece into place, keeping the tape on the back.

5. Hang your "stained-glass creation" in a window and see the light shining through!

The Cloisters

The Cloisters is a branch of the Museum, but it stands on a hilltop several miles away. It houses part of the Museum's medieval collection. Its architecture, statues, paintings, and church treasures reflect the life of the Middle Ages in Europe.

The Cuxa Cloister. From the Benedictine monastery of Saint-Michel-de-Cuxa, near Perpignan, France, about 1130–40. Marble.

Cloisters, covered passageways with open arches on one side overlooking a central garden, were part of medieval monasteries. Here monks could walk, think, read, and refresh the mind. They even shaved and did their laundry here.

The Cuxa Cloister is one of four reconstructed cloisters that make up the building. Most of the pink marble stonework was carved in the twelfth century. It is pieced together here from the ruins of a monastery in the Pyrenees (the mountains that separate France and Spain). In the cloister, light and shade play on the stone, fine carvings intrigue the eye, and the view through the arches changes with every step.

EYE SPY
What's unusual about the carved lions on this column? (Answer on page 72.)

Unicorn Tapestry

The Cloisters has a set of seven magnificent tapestries that tell the story of the Hunt of the Unicorn. The story is an allegory, full of symbols with heavenly and earthly meanings. People in the Middle Ages thought the unicorn symbolized both Jesus Christ, who Christians believe was slain and rose again, and a bridegroom captured by his lady love. The tapestries may have been made to celebrate a marriage.

EYE SPY
There are two initials that appear on this tapestry and all the others. What are they? (Answer on page 72.) The initials may be those of the newlyweds for whom the tapestries were made.

This tapestry shows the end of the story. The unicorn, which has been chased, captured, and killed, comes miraculously to life again. He is surrounded by flowers and fastened to the tree by the chain of love.

The tapestries were made about 1500 in the region that is now called Belgium. They were woven on giant looms prepared with long warp threads. The weavers threaded the wool, silk, and metallic weft threads under and over the warp threads by hand.

The Unicorn in Captivity. Franco-Flemish, about 1500. Tapestry: silk, wool, silver, and silver-gilt threads; 12 ft. 1 in. × 8 ft. 3 in.

FASCINATING FACT
It probably took a whole day for one weaver to complete one square inch of tapestry. We do not know how many weavers worked together, but the set of tapestries in The Cloisters contains 127,502 square inches. That was a lot of work!

Church Treasure

In the Middle Ages, relics or remains of saints were highly prized. Churches even competed to acquire bones, hair, teeth, or other fragments, for worshippers believed that relics made their prayers more effective. Such relics were kept in reliquaries. These were often fine works of art, created from the best materials to be worthy of their holy contents.

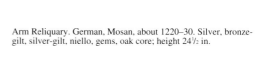

This reliquary, with its jewelled sleeve and golden fingers raised in blessing, probably contained the arm bone of a saintly bishop. Little windows, once covered with crystal, allowed glimpses of the relic.

Arm Reliquary. German, Mosan, about 1220–30. Silver, bronze-gilt, silver-gilt, niello, gems, oak core; height 24 1/2 in.

Armor of George Clifford, third Earl of Cumberland. English, Greenwich, about 1580–85. Steel, blued, etched, and gilded; height 69 1/2 in.

This tiny portrait shows the earl of Cumberland in his armor. It was painted by Nicholas Hilliard, an English artist, in about 1590. The portrait is at the Nelson-Atkins Museum of Art in Kansas City, Missouri.

THE DEPARTMENT OF ARMS AND ARMOR has more than 14,000 objects. Some of the weapons and pieces of protective armor were used in real battles; others were used in ceremonies. There is even armor for children and for horses!

Queen's Champion

The third earl of Cumberland was a handsome, brave, and adventurous Englishman who lived from 1558 to 1605. He was a great favorite of Queen Elizabeth I, who made him her Champion. In this office, he presided at grand tournaments, where knights showed off their skills before the queen. This magnificent armor, decorated with gold, was made for him at the royal armor workshops at Greenwich in the 1580s.

When the earl dressed in his armor, he had to put on fourteen separate pieces, fastened together with leather straps. Each piece was made of strong steel plates held together with rivets, or metal pins. This made the armor flexible and allowed the earl to move.

EYE SPY
How many places can you find where overlapping plates are riveted together to make bending possible? (Answer on page 72.)

YOUR TURN

Make your own movable armor.

1. Cut three strips of thin cardboard: one 3 inches x 12 inches and two 3 inches x 11 inches.

Etchers decorated the armor with royal emblems such as the Tudor rose, the fleur-de-lys, and the double *E* for Elizabeth. Then gilders colored the designs. The results were gorgeous, but the work was dangerous. Gold powder was mixed with mercury, letting off a gas that was poisonous to the gilders.

Tudor rose

In addition to making armor, armorers even went into battle with the knights to make on-the-spot repairs. They were the leading technologists of their day and were experts in design and in the use of metals. Many of their ideas have been used in later centuries. Early space suits had overlapping rings connecting the helmet to the collar. The design was based on armor like the earl of Cumberland's.

fleur-de-lys

double *E*

Design for a space helmet, 1963

BEHIND THE SCENES
The Metropolitan Museum has its own armor workshop. The armorers repair armor and replace lost parts, heating and hammering metal into shape in the traditional way. In addition to modern machinery, they use a set of old tools from Germany that have been handed down from generation to generation.

In the Arms and Armor Galleries, you can see a grand parade of knights on horseback.

2. Tape each strip into a ring.

3. Put each of the smaller rings into the larger ring, making an overlap of one inch.

4. Make holes through both of the rings on two sides and fasten the rings together with four brass paper fasteners.

5. Now put the tube around your elbow and see how much you can bend your arm.

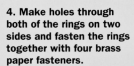

FASCINATING FACT
During World War II, the Museum's armor workshop was put to work for the United States Army. Helmets and protective jackets called flak jackets were designed here, using medieval armor for models.

Dōmaru (Armor).
Japanese, 16th and
18th centuries.
Lacquered iron
and leather, silk;
height 66 in.

Silk and Steel

The flame-colored armor on the left was probably worn by a very important samurai, a member of one of Japan's top warrior families. It was made in the eighteenth century in the style of earlier times. This Japanese armor was lighter, cooler, and more flexible than traditional European armor.

It is made of more than 4,500 small scales of steel and hardened leather, all laced together with leather thongs and silk braid.

The helmet, part of which was made in the sixteenth century, is decorated with gilded horns and a dreadful dragon. The helmet and the metal mask were designed to give protection and to frighten the enemy. The samurai's boots are covered with bear fur.

Japanese swords were sharp and deadly and very beautiful. Sword guards protected the hand from the blade. In Japan, ceremonial swords and sword guards are valued and admired as works of art.

Wakizashi (short sword).
Naotane, Japanese,
1778–1857. Steel,
length 20 in., 1839.

Tsuba (sword guard).
Ishiguro Masayoshi,
Japanese, about
1772–1869. Copper
alloys, gold, and
copper; 2⁷/₈ × 2⁵/₈ in.

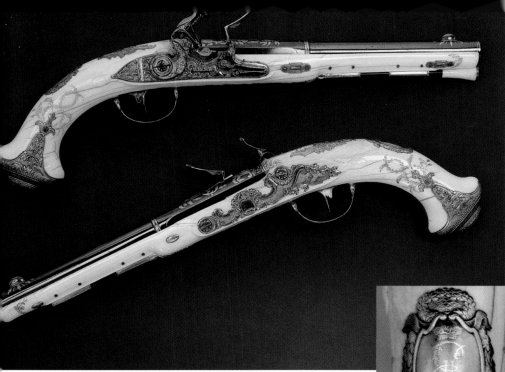

Pistols. Johann Adolf Grecke, Russian, 1755–1790. Steel, ivory, gold, brass; length, 14¼ in. each; 1786.

EYE SPY
Can you see the maker's name on the barrel?

Pistols for an Empress

These guns were made for Catherine the Great, the empress of Russia in the eighteenth century. They bear her monogram: a crown and an *E* for Ekaterine, her Russian name. They were made by Johann Adolf Grecke, the royal gunmaker.

These pistols, decorated with ivory, gold, and chiselled steel, were no ordinary guns. They belonged to a set of hunting guns, including a shotgun and a rifle. They were valued for the quality of the materials and the excellence of the craftsmanship, and they may never have been used. Catherine later gave them to her close friend, the king of Poland, as a special gift.

BEHIND THE SCENES
Most of the objects in the collections were purchased by the Museum or given by benefactors. These pistols came to the Museum in a very unusual way. Police found the guns during a raid and took them away with other stolen property. For ten years the pistols lay in a warehouse with other illegal guns. It was only when they were about to be destroyed that the police took a second look at them, then asked the Metropolitan Museum to take a look, too. Curators recognized what these guns were and put them on display. The owner from whom they had been stolen many years before was identified, and he decided to give the pistols permanently to the Museum.

The monogram of Catherine the Great

Catherine the Second, Empress of all the Russias.
William Dickinson after Virgilius Erichson.
Mezzotint, 18 x 13 in., 1773.

EYE SPY
Can you see a
crown and a sun-
burst on the desk
top? They are
symbols of the
Sun King.

Desk. Alexandre-
Jean Oppenordt,
French, 1639–1715.
Oak, pine, and walnut
veneered with
tortoiseshell, brass,
ebony, and rosewood;
height 30⁵/₁₆ in.,
width 41¾ in., depth
23³/₈ in., 1685.

THE WORKS IN THE DEPARTMENT OF EUROPEAN SCULPTURE AND DECORATIVE ARTS include things made by artists and artisans that people actually used—furniture, china and silver, and decorations. Many of the objects were made for palaces or great homes. There are even some entire rooms that have been reconstructed in the Museum.

From a Palace of the Sun King

Louis XIV, who ruled France from 1643 to 1715, was enormously rich, powerful, and proud. He was known as the Sun King, because his court was so magnificent. He surrounded himself with the very best of everything, from tapestries to paintings to furniture.

This room in the Museum has been decorated and filled with fine furnishings to show the magnificence of a grand bedroom at the time of Louis XIV. The objects in the room come from different places, but the writing desk belonged to the Sun King himself. It was one of a pair made for his study in the great palace of Versailles.

The desk is covered with red tortoiseshell. The tortoiseshell was cut with fine saws into small pieces. Then the pieces were fitted together with brass decorations, like a jigsaw puzzle. The completed design was glued to a wooden base.

Rolling Rider

This elegant ornament was made in Germany for a lavish home. Diana, goddess of the hunt, rides a gilded silver stag, but there is more to the object than meets the eye. It is an automaton, with a clockwork mechanism hidden in the base. When it was wound up, the automaton rolled around the table, much to everyone's amusement.

EYE SPY
Can you see where the stag's head and body come apart? In the seventeenth century, creatures like this one, with removable heads and hollow bodies, were used as luxurious drinking vessels.

Automaton: Diana on a Stag. Goldsmith work by Joachim Fries. German (Augsburg), about 1620. Silver, partially gilt, with a movement of iron and wood; height 14¾ in., width 9½ in.

The Works in the Department of the Arts of Africa, Oceania, and the Americas were made by the native peoples of Africa, the Pacific Islands (including Australia, New Zealand, Indonesia, New Guinea, and many others), and North and South America. Although their names are usually unknown, these artists were often highly skilled and well respected. They made these works for religious or ritual purposes, for practical use, or for personal adornment.

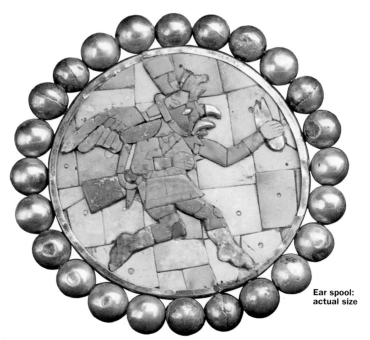

Ear spool: actual size

EYE SPY
Each ear spool is about 3½ inches across. How many pieces of colored stone and shell do you think were used to make each one? (Answer on page 72.)

Pair of Ear Spools. Peruvian, Moche, 3rd–6th centuries. Gold, stone, and shell; diameter 3½ in.

Golden Ears

The Moche people in Peru made this pair of ear spools hundreds of years ago. The Moche were skillful artisans; each ear plug is made of many tiny pieces of colored stone and shell, making a mosaic.

The mosaics show bird-headed human figures running along on booted feet and clutching bags in their outstretched hands. They may represent go-betweens who the Moche believed would carry messages between the supernatural world and the world of the living. The messengers' purpose is a mystery, lost in time. Yet the gold still glistens and the mosaics are alive with color.

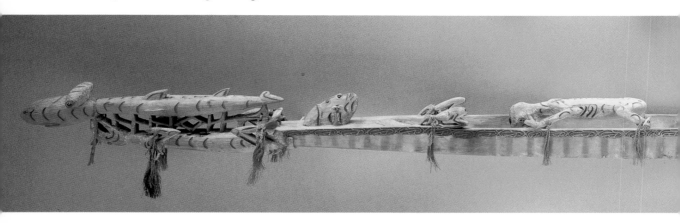

Soul Ship

Surrounded by trees and by water, the Asmat people of New Guinea traveled everywhere in wooden canoes. They were skilled at wood carving, and they believed that their carvings could help control spirit forces.

The canoe below is a soul ship. The 28-foot-long canoe, with its crew of human and animal spirits, was carved out of a single tree trunk. The canoe has no bottom, so the spirits seem to be gazing down into the depths below.

Soul ships never went into the water. They were built for ceremonies such as the initiation of boys into manhood. Each boy sat on the turtle near the center of the ship while special marks were cut on his body to give him strength.

A soul ship was also built if people thought that the dead were haunting their village. The ship was attacked in a make-believe fight and then left to rot in the jungle. The Asmat may have believed that it carried the souls back to the other world.

Canoes in Otsjanep, an Asmat village

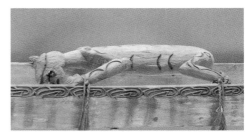

One of the soul ship's spirit figures

Soul Ship. Melanesian, Irian Jaya, 19th–20th centuries. Wood, length 28 1/2 ft.

EYE SPY
Can you find the turtle in the picture below?

Food for All

The Dogon people of West Africa have many myths about the creation of the world. One of these stories tells how, when the world was new, the creator god sent eight ancestors down from heaven. These ancestors traveled to earth in an ark like a grain basket, bringing everything the earth needed. The skills of work and the gifts of speech and dance came in the ark, along with mud to spread on fields, animals to help with work, seeds to scatter for crops, and a piece of the sun to make fire.

Thunderclaps sped the ark down a rainbow. It reached the earth with a bump, scattering its cargo of animals and plants in all directions. The ancestor who had guided the ark changed into a horse and pulled it across the dry land to precious water. The ancestors began their work.

Each year, when the Dogon harvest their grain, they pile food for a feast into a great wooden trough called the "ark of the world." The ark in the Museum is almost eight feet long and would hold enough food to feed a whole community. This feast is an offering to the creator god and the ancestors as well as a celebration of everyone's hard work.

Container with Horse's Head and Figures. African (Mali), Dogon, 16th–20th centuries. Wood, length 93 in.

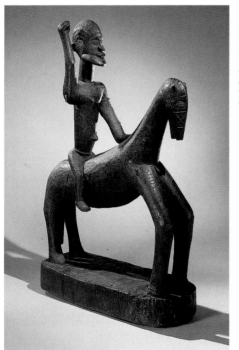

This sculpture shows a man riding a horse. Horses were signs of wealth and power among the Dogon people.

Horse and Rider. African (Mali), Dogon. 16th–20th centuries. Wood, height 27⅛ in.

This carved wooden figure shows a woman pounding grain to make flour. Sculptures like this one may have been made as visual prayers to the ancestors.

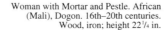

Woman with Mortar and Pestle. African (Mali), Dogon. 16th–20th centuries. Wood, iron; height 22¼ in.

EYE SPY
Can you see a
tongue-biting bird?

Rattle. Haida people,
Native American,
19th century. Wood,
pebbles, and paint;
length 13¾ in.

MUSICAL INSTRUMENTS make beautiful sounds, and they're often beautiful objects, as well. People all over the world express themselves in many musical languages, with many kinds of instruments.

Bird Rattle

This rattle was made in the nineteenth century by the Native American Haida people in the Pacific Northwest. It was part of the special equipment of a chief, who shook it in his outstretched hand as he danced a magical dance. The Haida people believed that the sounds made by the rattle communicated with the supernatural world.

The big black bird is a raven. On his back there is a carving of a man wearing an animal mask. A kingfisher bites the man's tongue, probably to pass on to him the magic powers of the animal spirits.

The wooden handle comes apart so that pebbles can be put inside. The rattle was decorated with paints made from plants and earth. Special, symbolic colors had to be used to give the rattle its magic.

YOUR TURN
Make a rattle.

1. Put a handful of rice, dried beans, or small stones into an empty plastic bottle, like a medicine bottle.

2. Put a wooden stick or a pencil into the opening of the bottle to make a handle. Tape the handle into place and tape the opening of the bottle closed.

3. Cover the bottle with colored paper.

4. Cut magical creatures out of paper or thin cardboard, paint them, and stick them onto your rattle.

Sweet Music

The virginal belongs to the harpsichord family, a group of instruments that was very popular in Europe before the piano was invented.

This double virginal was made in 1581 by Hans Rucker. The painting on the lid shows a party of elegant people enjoying themselves, and the Latin motto says, "Sweet music is a balm for toil."

The virginal has two keyboards: the "mother" on the right, and the higher pitched "child" on the left. When a key is pressed, the quill of a feather pulls on a piece of metal and makes it pluck a string. The child can be played separately, or it can be fitted above the mother so that her keys operate both sets of strings.

EYE SPY
Can you see the child in its drawer?

Double Virginal. Hans Rucker, Flemish, about 1545–1598. Painted wood; height 19½ in., width 71¾ in.; 1581.

The virginal closes up into a box that can be carried. One of its owners took it across the ocean to Peru, where it was discovered much later in a private chapel.

FASCINATING FACT
The Museum's huge collection of musical instruments includes the oldest piano in existence, made in 1720. Once in a while it is played, and its sounds are carried across the centuries to the ears of modern listeners.

Grand Piano. Bartolomeo Cristofori, Italian (Florence), 1655–1731. Wood and other materials, length 90 in., 1720.

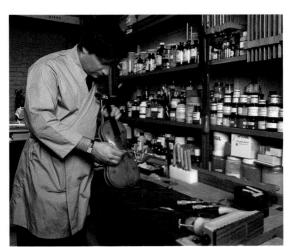

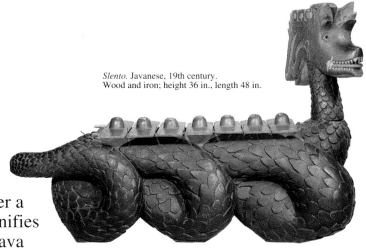

Slento. Javanese, 19th century.
Wood and iron; height 36 in., length 48 in.

Dragon and Peacock

Musical instruments have often been made in the shapes of animals.

The large scaly dragon is a metallophone. The bronze bars are struck with a wood or horn beater over a hollow in the dragon's back that magnifies the sound. The dragon was made in Java more than a hundred years ago.

The *mayūrī* (which means peacock) is a type of sitar, a popular Indian instrument. The one below was made in the nineteenth century.

The peacock keeps its feet on the ground while the end rests on the player's shoulder. The pegs adjust the sound of the strings that run along the fingerboard.

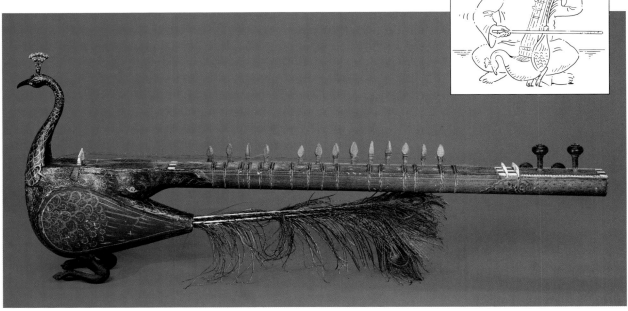

Mayūrī. Indian, 19th century. Wood, feathers, and other materials; length 44 in.

THE AMERICAN WING houses all kinds of art made in America by Americans, both in colonial times and since the founding of the United States. There are paintings, sculpture, furniture, silver and pewter, ceramics, and glass, as well as period rooms, which show how houses might have looked in the past.

Hart Room. American, Ipswich, Massachusetts, before 1674.

Well Built and Well Furnished

The colonists who settled in New England in the 1630s had left their homes and their furniture behind when they came to the New World. With a few tools and the materials they found around them they started all over again. By 1642 Edward Johnson was able to write that all the "wigwams, huts and hovels" had been turned into "orderly, fair and well-built houses, well-furnished many of them."

Thomas Hart, a tanner by trade, built a house in Ipswich, Massachusetts, in about 1670. The main room or hall would have been used for cooking, eating, sitting, and sleeping. This room, with its wooden beams and open fireplace, is now in the Museum.

The seventeenth-century furniture is solidly made from oak and pine, with carved legs and panels for decoration.

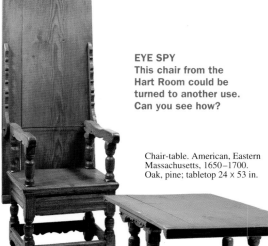

EYE SPY
This chair from the Hart Room could be turned to another use. Can you see how?

Chair-table. American, Eastern Massachusetts, 1650–1700. Oak, pine; tabletop 24 x 53 in.

Sculpture in the Round

In this nineteenth-century sculpture of two mythological characters, *Bacchante and Infant Faun,* the laughing girl dances around, teasing the baby whose eyes are fixed on the circling grapes.

The girl is perfectly balanced on the toes of one foot. The sculptor, Frederick MacMonnies, made quite sure she would not topple over.

When you walk around a sculpture like this one, you can make a moving picture for yourself. The outline alters as you change your viewpoint. You can never take in a sculpture with a single glance. It is made to be looked at from all directions.

EYE SPY
Imagine a line going straight up from the center of the statue's base. Can you see how the weight of the sculpture falls equally on either side?

Bacchante and Infant Faun.
Frederick William MacMonnies, American, 1863–1937. Bronze, height 83 in.

front view   back view

Tiffany Glass

Louis Comfort Tiffany loved making beautiful objects from glass. He experimented with new methods and produced glass in thousands of different colors.

This lamp was made in his New York Studios in about 1910, when electricity was just coming into use in people's homes. The lamp contains ten small bulbs, whose light glows through the petals and bamboo stems on the lotus-flower shade and lights up the bronze lily-pad base.

The lampshade is made of dozens of pieces of clear and cloudy glass held together with lead. Tiffany's technique was similar to the one used by the medieval glassmakers on page 33. In fact, Tiffany was also famous for windows, like the one on the right.

Table Lamp. American, Tiffany Studios, New York. Leaded-glass with bronze base; height 26 1/2 in., diameter 18 1/2 in.; about 1910.

Autumn Landscape.
Tiffany Studios, New York. Panel from a leaded-glass window, 1923.

Washington Crossing the Delaware

On Christmas night in 1776, George Washington and his troops crossed the Delaware River under cover of darkness. They traveled in heavy, flat-bottomed boats, followed by their horses. Progress was slow, because there was a heavy snowstorm and thin ice floated on the water. After a nine-mile march they reached Trenton just as daylight was breaking. Here they found the enemy just finishing their Christmas celebrations, caught them by surprise, and won the Battle of Trenton. This success, under Washington's leadership, was a turning point on the way to victory in the Revolutionary War.

Washington Crossing the Delaware. Emanuel Leutze, American, 1816–1868.
Oil on canvas, 12 ft. 5 in. x 21 ft. 3 in., 1851.

Seventy-five years later, Emanuel Leutze painted this picture of the crossing. Every picture tells a story, and this story is a true one, but Leutze was not worried about getting all the details right.

Washington would have fallen over if he had tried to stand up like this in a small boat on a stormy night. Leutze painted him in this position to make him look brave, determined, and ready for action.

The Stars and Stripes did not become America's flag until 1777, but Leutze included it as a symbol of the colonists' struggle for freedom.

IN THE EUROPEAN PAINTINGS DEPARTMENT you'll find works of art from the thirteenth through the nineteenth centuries, including great paintings from the Italian Renaissance to French Impressionism.

Three Miracles of Saint Zenobius. Sandro Botticelli, Italian (Florentine), 1444/45–1510. Tempera on wood, 26¹/₂ x 59¹/₄ in.

Miracles in Paint

Sandro Botticelli lived in the Italian city of Florence in the second half of the fifteenth century. This painting shows three miracles being performed by Saint Zenobius, a fifth-century bishop who became the patron saint of Florence.

Zenobius appears three times in the painting. You can recognize him by his triangular bishop's hat or miter. In the first two scenes he is bringing people back to life. In the third, he is blessing water, which is taken away to revive another dead person.

EYE SPY
If the lines along the side walls of the buildings continued into the distance, where would they meet? This imaginary meeting place is known as the vanishing point.

Botticelli, like other artists at the time, was fascinated by perspective, the means of representing space and distance on a flat surface. Here the lines of the buildings lead your eyes forward to the miracles in the foreground and back toward the far-off hills.

The Harvesters. Pieter Bruegel the Elder, Flemish, active by 1551, d. 1569. Oil on wood, 46½ x 63¼ in, 1565.

The Harvesters

It is a hot summer day. Men and women have been hard at work for hours, cutting the ripe grain with scythes then binding it into sheaves to dry. The golden harvest stretches on into the distance, but now, for a moment, the peasants can rest and gossip and devour their midday meal.

Pieter Bruegel painted this picture in the sixteenth century. It was one of a series of paintings he made showing the activities of different seasons or months of the year.

Bruegel composed the painting to make it pleasing to the eye. Notice how the group on the right balances the distant view on the left, with the diagonal sweep of golden grain dividing the two parts.

You can wend your way through the fields with your eyes, discovering unexpected details on the way. Can you figure out what the people you see are doing?

EYE SPY
Can you see what happened to the grain after it was cut?

Goya's Children

In about 1788, the Spanish artist Francisco Goya painted this portrait of a small boy, about four years old. Goya worked for the king of Spain, and he painted many pictures of the Spanish nobility, including this boy and his family.

The child's solemn, wide-eyed expression and stunning costume catch your attention immediately. His innocent face is lit up in contrast with the menacing darkness behind him where three cats fix greedy eyes on his pet magpie.

EYE SPY
Can you see the child's name, Don Manuel Osorio Manrique de Zuñiga, at the bottom of the painting? Can you find the artist's name? (Answer on page 72.)

Don Manuel Osorio Manrique de Zuñiga. Francisco de Goya y Lucientes, Spanish, 1746–1828. Oil on canvas, 50 × 40 in.

Goya had many children, but only one of them lived to be an adult. He adored his son and, later, his grandson. It was unusual at this time to paint pictures of children, but Goya understood children and loved painting them. He always liked to include pets or favorite toys in his portraits.

Pepito, painted in about 1813, poses seriously in his finery, but it is easy to imagine him leaping onto his hobbyhorse or waking everyone up with his drum.

José Costa y Bonells, called Pepito. Francisco de Goya y Lucientes, Spanish, 1746–1828. Oil on canvas, 41³/₈ × 33¹/₄ in.

Beneath the Surface

In the Museum's Paintings Conservation Department, conservators clean and restore paintings to preserve them for the future. It is painstaking work that has to be done very carefully. Conservators remove dirt and old varnish. They also repair cracked and flaking paint to prevent further damage.

There is more to a painting than meets the eye. Through scientific studies, conservators are able to explore the layers beneath the surface without disturbing them. X-rays can reveal information about working techniques, particularly the brushwork in areas where the artist used lead-white paint. Infrared reflectography can penetrate the paint layers to reveal an early drawing in works done on wooden panels. Autoradiography shows the artist's progress at different stages of the painting process. Sometimes it can reveal a sketch underneath a painting on canvas.

A paintings conservator retouches tiny paint losses.

On the monitor, infrared reflectography reveals the underdrawing in the head of one figure.

When Anthony van Dyck's painting of Saint Rosalie was investigated, one autoradiograph revealed a big surprise: an upside-down portrait of the artist underneath the picture of Saint Rosalie! Van Dyck had drawn himself before turning the canvas around and using it again.

Saint Rosalie Interceding for the Plague-stricken of Palermo. Anthony van Dyck, Flemish, 1599–1641. Oil on canvas, 39¹/₄ x 29 in.

EYE SPY
Turn the picture upside-down to see how van Dyck saw himself.

Making an Impression

In France about a hundred years ago, a group of artists explored new ways of using their eyes and their paint-brushes. The Impressionists, as they came to be called, were fascinated by the effect of light on colors and shapes. In their paintings, they tried to capture an impression of what they saw rather than an exact likeness.

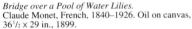

Bridge over a Pool of Water Lilies.
Claude Monet, French, 1840–1926. Oil on canvas, 36¹/₂ × 29 in., 1899.

Monet loved his garden at Giverny. With streaks and flecks of color, he conjured up trees, water, and flowers in his painting of the lily pool.

Rouen Cathedral: The Portal (in Sun). Claude Monet, French, 1840–1926. Oil on canvas, 39¹/₄ × 25⁷/₈ in., 1894.

Rouen Cathedral is made of solid stone, but when Claude Monet looked at it, he found that its appearance changed with every change in the light. It even looked soft and hazy at certain times of day. He was so fascinated that he painted the cathedral more than thirty times at different times of day. This painting was done at midday. Monet built up the sunlit surfaces of the stone with thick layers of paint in an array of colors. If you move back from the painting, you can see dark smudges turn into misty shadows, bringing the outlines of the stonework into focus.

Other artists found different ways of interpreting what they saw.

Georges Seurat used dots of pure color in this dreamlike painting of a musical sideshow viewed by gaslight. If you look closely, the dots of color form an overall pattern. From further back, the shapes of the people, the lights, and the building emerge.

EYE SPY
When you look at this small section from Seurat's painting, you see the dabs of bright color. Can you find where this area belongs in the painting? (Answer on page 72.)

Circus Sideshow. Georges Seurat, French, 1859–1891. Oil on canvas, 39¼ × 59 in., 1887–88.

Cypresses. Vincent van Gogh, Dutch, 1853–1890. Oil on canvas, 36¾ × 29⅛ in., 1889.

Vincent van Gogh loved the look of these trees standing like statues in the sunshine. He worked hard to find the right colors for their dark shapes. His swirling brushstrokes breathe life and movement into his impression of the scene.

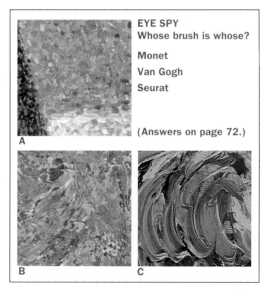

EYE SPY
Whose brush is whose?

Monet

Van Gogh

Seurat

(Answers on page 72.)

A

B   C

THE COSTUME INSTITUTE has more than 40,000 examples of the finest clothes made and worn in the last 400 years. This huge collection includes many of the fashions that can be seen in paintings. Delicate fabrics cannot be left on display for long, so the costume exhibitions change frequently. When costumes are not on exhibition they are stored away carefully to preserve them for the future.

Costume storage

Decorated Dresses

The magnificent dress on the right was made for a French lady in the eighteenth century. It has two separate parts: a full-length robe that opens down the front over a "petticoat" of the same material. Once the dressmaker had made the dress it was the job of the milliner to design and sew on all the trimmings.

EYE SPY
Can you see how strips of ribbon have been used to create the patterns on the petticoat?

Dress. French, about 1760. Lavender-pink brocaded silk.

Throughout the world people have always liked to decorate the clothes they wear. The costume of a Miao woman from Southeast Asia is patterned with fine stitching. The baby carrier she wears on her back is intricately embroidered.

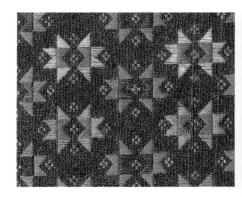

Miao Woman's Jacket, Skirt, and Baby Carrier. Chinese, Guizhou Province, second half of the 20th century. Embroidered cotton.

Doublet Fashion

Doublets such as this one were the height of fashion for wealthy young men in Europe in the early seventeenth century. The upper chest and sleeves were made of strips called panes that allowed the billowing shirt worn underneath to show through. A painting by Frans Hals in the Museum's collection shows a simpler version of a doublet like this one.

Doublet. European, about 1625. Ivory silk woven in a colored floral pattern.
The Smoker. Frans Hals, Dutch, born after 1580–1666. Oil on wood, 18⅜ × 19½ in.

EYE SPY
Can you see the holes along the waist seam? What are they for? (Answer on page 72.)

BEHIND THE SCENES
The doublet is nearly four hundred years old. When it came to the Museum it needed treatment. Using fine silk thread dyed to match the fabric, conservators reinforced the worn areas to prevent further tears.

Growing Up

Before the twentieth century, boys and girls were dressed alike until they were about five or six years old. Then boys were breeched, which means they were given trousers to wear. We know this white embroidered dress and pantalettes belonged to a little boy who lived in New York in 1841. The Museum has a portrait of his family that shows him wearing them.

Boy's Dress. American, 1841. White cotton.

This older boy's "skeleton suit" is in the same style as the suits worn by the children painted by Goya on page 54. It has lots of buttons to keep it tidily together, but it is loose enough to allow plenty of room to move. It was a popular style for small boys from the late eighteenth century to the beginning of the twentieth century.

James Abel Williamson Family. John Mix Stanley, American, 1814–1872. Oil on canvas, 27 × 22 in., about 1841–42.

These sisters' dresses are shorter versions of styles their mother wore.

Young Boy's Skeleton Suit. English, 1796–1800. Cotton.

Young Girls' Dresses. American, about 1885. Heavy ribbed silk.

DRAWINGS, PHOTOGRAPHS, PRINTS, AND ILLUSTRATED BOOKS are referred to as works on paper. The Museum has over one million of these works, in several different departments. Works on paper become faded and fragile if they are exposed to too much light, so exhibitions are changed frequently. These are some of the kinds of pictures you might see on view.

Studies for the Libyan Sibyl.
Michelangelo Buonarroti, Italian,
1475–1564. Red chalk, 11³/₈ × 8⁷/₁₆ in.

EYE SPY
Can you see how
Michelangelo made ridges
and hollows by shading?

**The final version of
the *Libyan Sibyl* from
the Sistine Chapel**

Drawings: Michelangelo's Model

Sometimes artists make drawings as sketches or designs for paintings, sculpture, or other works. Sometimes they make drawings as finished works of art.

Michelangelo Buonarroti was fascinated by the beauty and power of the human body. He studied anatomy and even dissected corpses to discover the workings of bones, joints, and muscles. He observed live models and made drawings to perfect his skill.

In 1508, at the request of Pope Julius II, Michelangelo began painting the ceiling of the Sistine Chapel in Rome. He filled its huge expanse with scenes from the Bible and from antiquity. He made this drawing from real life in preparation for painting one of the figures.

Using red chalk on paper, Michelangelo molded each contour of the body with light and shade. He probably licked the chalk to make the darkest patches.

Photographs: Alice in Wonderland

Alice Liddell was the real Alice who inspired Lewis Carroll's *Alice in Wonderland*. This photograph of her was taken in 1872, when she was a young woman and photography was still a new art form. Photographs can reproduce things as they actually appear, but here Julia Margaret Cameron used her imagination to pose Alice as Flora, the Roman goddess of flowers, the way a painter might use a model.

Alice Liddell.
Julia Margaret Cameron,
British, 1815–1879.
Albumen silver print
from glass negative,
14¹/₄ × 10¹/₄ in., 1872.

Prints: Dürer Endures

In 1515, Albrecht Dürer drew this rhinoceros, and then he carved it into a block of wood and printed it onto paper. Many copies were printed.

Dürer had never actually seen a rhinoceros. One had been brought to Europe, but it drowned while being shipped from Portugal to Italy. Dürer had to use his imagination to turn other people's descriptions into a picture. Do you think it looks like a real rhinoceros?

Even if you have never seen a rhinoceros yourself, you have probably seen plenty of photographs in books or on television. Before photography and television, people relied on artists to show them the appearance of famous people, cities, works of art, and other things

The Rhinoceros. Albrecht Dürer, German, 1471–1528. Woodcut, 8 3/8 × 11 5/8 in., 1515.

they could not see for themselves. Images like this one could be printed many times and the pictures could be made widely available.

Dürer's print continued to be reproduced for 200 years, as no one had come up with a better picture of a rhinoceros. It was even copied on this French snuff box and this English platter, both made in the middle of the eighteenth century.

Platter with Rhinoceros. England, Chelsea, about 1752–54. Soft-paste porcelain, 9 3/4 × 12 3/4 in.

Snuff Box. French (Paris), 1768–69. Gold; length 3 3/16 in., width 2 5/16 in., height 1 1/8 in.

BEHIND THE SCENES
Behind the scenes, there are study rooms where scholars and experts from around the world come to work. Here they can examine drawings, photographs, prints, and illustrated books that cannot be put on public display.

The Museum's Collection of Twentieth-Century Art is housed in the galleries of the Lila Acheson Wallace Wing. The collections include everything from paintings, sculpture, and drawings to chairs, lamps, and pepper mills.

Leaping Lines

Arms, legs, and bodies bend, twist, and leap all over *Handbill for Comedians* by Paul Klee. With a few black lines the artist sets a carnival in motion. You can think of comics in funny hats or their leaping, dancing limbs. Or you can just enjoy the mazelike pattern. Klee painted *Handbill* on a sheet of newsprint in 1938.

Handbill for Comedians. Paul Klee, German, 1879–1940. Gouache on newsprint, 19$\frac{1}{8}$ × 12$\frac{5}{8}$ in., 1938.

> **YOUR TURN**
>
> **Make a "Handbill."**
>
> Think of the movements athletes make when they are throwing, running, or jumping, or think of children skipping, dancing, and doing handstands. Simplify these actions into lines, then use a thick black felt-tip pen to draw the lines onto a large sheet of paper. Try to arrange the lines to make a pleasing pattern.

Paint Patterns

Jackson Pollock started out making realistic works, like the drawing of a young girl below. Then, as his work developed, he became more interested in abstract patterns created by chance.

When Pollock painted *Autumn Rhythm* in October 1950, he laid his canvas on the floor and dripped, poured, flicked, and spattered the paint onto it. Yet from end to end of the enormous canvas he never allowed the rhythm of lines and spots and colors to run out of his control.

Girl with Braids. Jackson Pollock, American, 1912–1956. Colored pencils and graphite on paper, 22$\frac{1}{2}$ × 14$\frac{1}{4}$ in., about 1938–39.

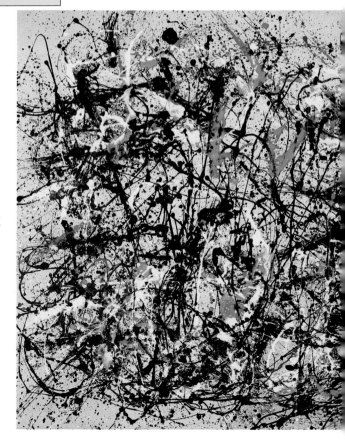

Colored Squares

Chuck Close took a photograph of his friend Lucas (below, right). He drew a grid of lines over the photograph then enlarged the grid of more than 3,000 squares onto a big canvas. Following the squares on the photograph, he carefully filled in each square on the canvas with paint. Just as he planned it, the separate squares of color merge to form a huge portrait of Lucas (below, left).

Study for Lucas. Chuck Close, American, b. 1940. Photograph, pencil, and tape pasted on cardboard; 29 x 24 in.; 1987.

In the nineteenth century, artists such as Seurat explored the use of strokes of pure color, instead of shading or blending, to create an overall impression (see page 57). A century later, this exploration has been taken still further by Chuck Close.

Lucas. Chuck Close, American, b. 1940. Oil and pencil on canvas, 100 x 84 in., 1986–87.

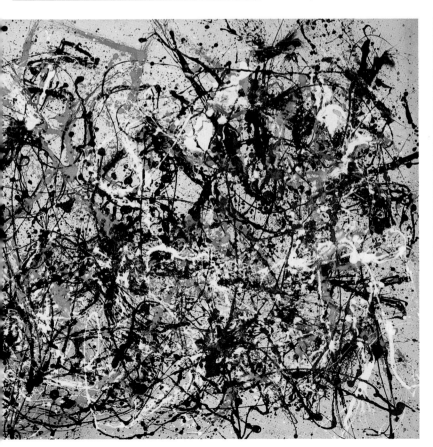

Jackson Pollock (with painting No. 32). Hans Namuth, American, b. Germany, 1915. Gelatin silver photograph, 19$\frac{1}{8}$ x 15$\frac{1}{4}$ in., 1950.

Autumn Rhythm. Jackson Pollock, American, 1912–1956. Oil on canvas, 105 x 207 in., 1950.

The Figure 5 in Gold

This painting is about a person, William Carlos Williams, and the poem he wrote after seeing a fire truck one dark night.

Williams wanted his words to make pictures. Read the poem, "The Great Figure," slowly. What do you see in your mind's eye?

Charles Demuth was Williams's friend. He painted the images the poem conjured up in his mind. The golden figure 5 echoes through the night as the red fire truck rushes on.

The Great Figure

Among the rain
and lights
I saw the figure 5
in gold
on a red
firetruck
moving
tense
unheeded
to gong clangs
siren howls
and wheels rumbling
through the dark city.

EYE SPY
Demuth painted the picture in honor of his friend. Can you find three references to the name William Carlos Williams in the painting? (Answers on page 72.)

The Figure 5 in Gold. Charles Demuth, American, 1883–1935. Oil on cardboard, 35½ x 30 in., 1928.

Becca. David Smith, American, 1906–1965. Stainless steel, height 113¼ in., width 123 in., depth 30½ in., 1965.

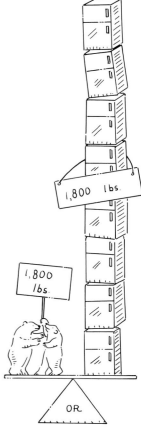

FASCINATING FACT
Becca is ten feet long and almost as high. It weighs 1,800 pounds, as much as two polar bears or eight refrigerators!

Becca

The sculpture by MacMonnies on page 49 was made by pouring liquid bronze into a mold. Many sculptures in the Museum were made by carving marble or other stone.

David Smith was the first American to make sculptures by welding pieces of metal together. *Becca* is named after Smith's daughter, but it is not intended to be a portrait. It is an abstract arrangement of huge stainless-steel plates that form a graceful, balanced shape, meant to be viewed from the front. Playful scribbles dance across the surface of the steel, adding energy and liveliness to the mass of metal.

The Burghers of Calais. Auguste Rodin, French, 1840–1917. Bronze; height 82½ in.; modeled 1884–95, cast 1985.

BEHIND THE SCENES
There is a sculpture garden on top of the Museum. Some sculptures are so large that the Museum's movers have to use a crane to hoist them from ground level up to the roof! Then they are moved into place with a device called an A-frame.

This room at the Museum (above) looks almost the way it did in the Lehmans' house (right).

THE ROBERT LEHMAN COLLECTION is a museum in a museum. The Lehman family loved fine paintings, furniture, and sculpture. They filled their New York town house with great works of art. When Robert Lehman died, he left the whole collection to the Museum, where a new wing was built to house it. Some of the galleries are modeled on the Lehman house: Sumptuous velvet, elegant furniture, and elaborately carved wood recall the surroundings in which the Lehmans enjoyed their cherished collection.

A Pair of Portraits

The treasures in the Lehman Collection include a pair of portraits of a husband and wife, painted in Italy in the late fifteenth century. The backgrounds of the two paintings match up. Can you see the Latin inscription UT SIT NOSTRA FORMA SUPERSTES running across the building in both paintings? It means "So that our images may survive," and so they have,

Matteo Gozzadini and *Ginevra Lupari*. Italian (Emilian), 15th century. Tempera on panel, 20 x 14 1/2 in. each.

ending up 500 years later in a Museum 4,000 miles away from the country where they were created.

Two Young Girls at the Piano. Pierre-Auguste Renoir, French, 1841–1919. Oil on canvas, 44 x 34 in., 1892.

All Wrapped Up

The French artist Pierre-Auguste Renoir believed that paintings were for looking at, rather than talking about. "If they could explain a picture it wouldn't be art....The work of art must seize upon you, wrap you up in itself, carry you away."

The Lehmans well understood this feeling of becoming "wrapped up" in a painting, seeing more and feeling more as they looked and looked again. The Lehman Collection is designed to share this opportunity with everyone.

Renoir was one of Robert Lehman's favorite artists, and the collection includes many examples of his work, including *Two Young Girls at the Piano*, painted in 1892. Take a long look at this painting, from close up and from further away, letting your eyes wander across it and focus on details. You may even find it beginning to wrap you up and carry you away!

The works of art featured in this book were made over thousands of years, in many different parts of the world. Match each object to its place in the world and its date on the timeline, and put the letters into the correct circles. The answers are on page 72.

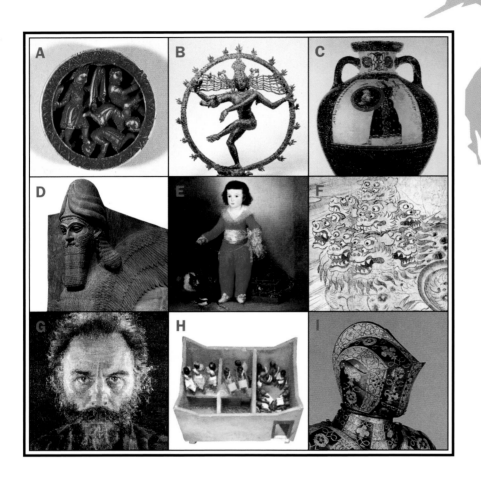

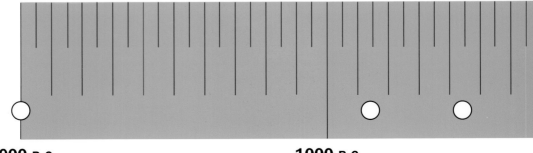

2000 B.C.   1000 B.C.

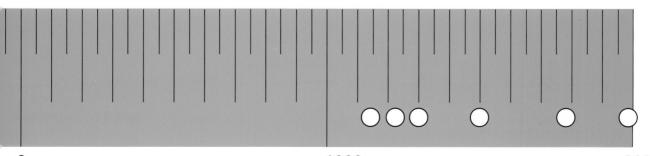

p. 8: Seated Female Figurine. Gift of Sheldon and Barbara Breitbart, 1985   1985.356.32

p. 9: *Water Stone.* Isamu Noguchi, American, 1904-1988. Black basalt. Purchase, Anonymous Gift, 1987   1987.222

p. 10: Garland Sarcophagus. Gift of Abdo Debbas, 1870   70.1

p. 15: Turban Helmet. Purchase, Anonymous Gift, 1950   50.87

p. 15: Violin. Gift of George Gould, 1955   55.86a

p. 16: Outer Coffin of Henettawy. Rogers Fund, 1925   25.3.182

p. 17: Temple of Dendur. Given to the United States by Egypt in 1965, awarded to The Metropolitan Museum of Art
   in 1967, and installed in The Sackler Wing in 1978   68.154

p. 18: Ancient Model of a Bearer. Rogers Fund and Edward S. Harkness Gift, 1920   20.3.7

p. 19: Ancient Model of a Granary. Rogers Fund and Edward S. Harkness Gift, 1920   20.3.11

pp. 18–19: Ancient Model of a Traveling Boat. Rogers Fund and Edward S. Harkness Gift, 1920   20.3.1

p. 20: Necklace and Pectoral. Purchase, Rogers Fund and Henry Walters Gift, 1916   16.1.3

p. 21: Coffin of Nephthys. Rogers Fund, 1911   11.150.15

p. 21: Hippopotamus. Gift of Edward S. Harkness, 1917   17.9.1

p. 22: Human-headed Winged Lion. Gift of John D. Rockefeller, Jr., 1932   32.143.2

p. 22: Relief of a Winged Deity. Gift of John D. Rockefeller, Jr., 1932   32.143.7

p. 23: Nubian Tribute Bearer. Rogers Fund, 1960   60.145.11

p. 23: Plate 2 from *Monuments of Ninevah I.* Rogers Fund

pp. 24–25: *Wang Hsi-chih Watching Geese.* Gift of the Dillon Fund, 1973   1973.120.6

p. 24: Seal Paste Box. H. O. Havemeyer Collection, Bequest of Mrs. H. O. Havemeyer, 1929   29.100.358ab
   Tortoise Seal. Gift of Robert James Sistrunk, 1982   1982.203
   Bamboo Seal. Gift of A. W. Bahr, 1958   58.64.17

p. 24: *Tenjin Engi.* Fletcher Fund, 1925   25.224d

p. 25: *Shiva Nataraja.* Harris Brisbane Dick Fund, 1964   64.251

pp. 26–27: The Astor Court, made possible by The Vincent Astor Foundation

p. 28: Prayer Niche. Harris Brisbane Dick Fund, 1939   39.20

p. 28: Pair of Doors. Edward C. Moore Collection, Bequest of Edward C. Moore, 1891   91.1.2064 a,b

p. 29: Tiles. Rogers Fund, 1922   22.185.13a-f

p. 29: Rug. Bequest of Joseph V. McMullan, 1973   1974.149.29

p. 29: *Prince Riding an Elephant.* Rogers Fund, 1925   25.68.4

p. 30: Panathenaic Prize Amphora. Classical Purchase Fund, 1978   1978.11.13

p. 31: Chariot. Rogers Fund, 1903   03.23.1

p. 31: Amphora. Fletcher Fund, 1956   56.171.9

p. 32: Hanging Lamp. Fletcher Fund, 1962   62.10.1

p. 32: Game Piece, Hercules. Rogers Fund, 1916   16.106

p. 32: Game Piece, Samson. Gift of J. Pierpont Morgan, 1917   17.190.141

p. 32: Box. Purchase, Gift of J. Pierpont Morgan, by exchange, 1976   1976.327

p. 33: *The Nativity.* Francis F. Leland Fund, 1913   13.64.4

p. 33: *The Glazier.* From Hartman Schopper's *Panoplia Omnium Illiberatium Mechanicum avt Sedentariarum...*, Frankfurt, 1568.
   Harris Brisbane Dick Fund, 1930   30.48.4

p. 34: The Cuxa Cloister. The Cloisters Collection, 1925   25.120

p. 35: *The Unicorn in Captivity.* The Cloisters Collection, 1937   37.80.6

p. 35: Arm Reliquary. The Cloisters Collection, 1947   47.101.33

p. 36: Armor of George Clifford. Munsey Fund, 1932   32.130.6

p. 36: *George Clifford, Earl of Cumberland.* Nicholas Hilliard, English, 1546-1619. Watercolor, $2\frac{3}{4} \times 2\frac{1}{4}$ in., ca. 1590.
   The Nelson-Atkins Museum of Art, Kansas City, Missouri (Gift of Mr. and Mrs. John W. Starr through
   the Starr Foundation) F58-60/188.

p. 37: Design for a Space Helmet. Detail from "Dressing for Space," from *Nature and Science*, October 4, 1963.
   Courtesy of Doubleday.

p. 38: *Dōmaru.* Rogers Fund, 1904   04.4.2

p. 38: *Wakizashi.* Gift of Brayton Ives and W. T. Walters, 1891   91.2.84

p. 38: *Tsuba.* The Howard Mansfield Collection, Gift of Howard Mansfield, 1936   36.120.79

p. 39: Pair of Pistols. Gift of John M. Schiff, 1986   1986.265.1, 2

p. 39: *Catherine the Second, Empress of all the Russias.* Bequest of Susan Dwight Bliss, 1966   67.630.1

p. 40: Desk. Gift of Mrs. Charles Wrightsman, 1986   1986.365.3

p. 41: Automaton. Gift of J. Pierpont Morgan, 1917   17.190.746

p. 42: Ear Spools. Gift and Bequest of Alice K. Bache, 1966, 1977   66.196.40,41

p. 43: Otsjanep Village, Asmat People, Irian Jaya, Melanesia. Photograph by Tobias Schneebaum. The Photograph Study Collection, Department
   of the Arts of Africa, Oceania, and the Americas.

pp. 42–43: Soul Ship. The Michael C. Rockefeller Memorial Collection, Bequest of Nelson A. Rockefeller, 1979   1979.206.1558

p. 44: Container with Horse's Head and Figures. The Michael C. Rockefeller Memorial Collection, Bequest of Nelson A. Rockefeller, 1979
   1979.206.255

p. 44: Horse and Rider. The Michael C. Rockefeller Memorial Collection, Bequest of Nelson A. Rockefeller, 1979   1979.206.85

p. 44: Woman with Mortar and Pestle. Gift of Lester Wunderman, 1977   1979.541.12

p. 45: Rattle. The Crosby Brown Collection of Musical Instruments, 1889   89.4.615

p. 46: Double Virginal. Gift of B. H. Homan, 1929   29.90
p. 46: Grand Piano. The Crosby Brown Collection of Musical Instruments, 1889   89.4.1219
p. 47: *Slento*. The Crosby Brown Collection of Musical Instruments, 1889   89.4.1462
p. 47: *Mayūrī*. The Crosby Brown Collection of Musical Instruments, 1889   89.4.163
p. 48: Hart Room. Munsey Fund, 1936   36.127
p. 48: Chair-table. Gift of Mrs. Russell Sage, 1909   10.125.697
p. 49: *Bacchante and Infant Faun*. Gift of Charles F. McKim, 1897   97.19
p. 49: Table Lamp. Gift of Hugh J. Grant, 1974   1974.214.15ab
p. 49: *Autumn Landscape*. Gift of Robert W. DeForest, 1925   25.173
pp. 50-51: *Washington Crossing the Delaware*. Gift of John Stewart Kennedy, 1897   97.34
p. 52: *Three Miracles of Saint Zenobius*. John Stewart Kennedy Fund, 1911   11.98
p. 53: *The Harvesters*. Rogers Fund, 1919   19.164
p. 54: *Don Manuel Osorio Manrique de Zuñiga*. The Jules Bache Collection, 1949   49.7.41
p. 54: *José Costa y Bonells, called Pepito*. Gift of Countess Bismarck, 1961   61.259
p. 55: *Saint Rosalie Interceding for the Plague-stricken of Palermo*. Purchase, 1871   71.41
p. 56: *Rouen Cathedral: The Portal (in Sun)*. Theodore M. Davis Collection, Bequest of Theodore M. Davis, 1915   30.95.250
p. 56: *Bridge over a Pool of Water Lilies*. H. O. Havemeyer Collection, Bequest of Mrs. H. O. Havemeyer, 1929   29.100.113
p. 57: *Circus Sideshow*. Bequest of Stephen C. Clark, 1960   61.101.17
p. 57: *Cypresses*. Rogers Fund, 1949   49.30
p. 58: Dress. Purchase, Irene Lewisohn Bequest, 1959   CI 59.29.1ab
p. 58: Miao Woman's Jacket, Skirt, and Baby Carrier. Purchase, Irene Lewisohn Bequest, 1987   1987.100.2
p. 59: Doublet. Purchase, The Costume Institute Fund, in memory of Polaire Weissman, 1989   1989.196
p. 59: *The Smoker*. Marquand Collection, Gift of Henry G. Marquand, 1889   89.15.34
p. 59: Boy's Dress. Gift of George H. Danforth, 1976   1976.363
p. 59: *James Abel Williamson Family*. Gift of George H. Danforth, 1976   1976.338
p. 59: Young Boy's Skeleton Suit. Isabel Shults Fund, 1986   1986.106.14
p. 59: Young Girls' Dresses. Gifts of Charlotte Church Collins, in memory of her mother, Alice Slocum Church, 1976   1976.257.1ab, .2ab
p. 60: *Studies for the Libyan Sibyl*. Purchase, Joseph Pulitzer Bequest, 1924   24.197.2
p. 60: Libyan Sibyl. Sistine Chapel, Vatican
p. 60: *Alice Liddell*. David Hunter McAlpin Fund, 1963   63.545
p. 61: *The Rhinoceros*. Gift of Junius S. Morgan, 1919   19.73.159
p. 61: Snuff Box. Gift of Mr. and Mrs. Charles Wrightsman, 1976   1976.155.17
p. 61: Platter with Rhinoceros. Gift of Irwin Untermyer, 1964   64.101.482
p. 62: *Handbill for Comedians*. The Berggruen Klee Collection, 1984   1984.315.57
p. 62: *Girl with Braids*. Gift of Lee Krasner Pollock, 1982   1982.147.7
pp. 62-63: *Autumn Rhythm*. George A. Hearn Fund, 1957   57.92
p. 63: *Lucas*. Purchase, Lila Acheson Wallace Gift and Gift of Arnold and Milly Glimcher, 1987   1987.282
p. 63: *Study for Lucas*. Gift of Leslie and Chuck Close, 1987   1987.329
p. 63: *Jackson Pollock (with painting No. 32)*. Purchase, Warner Communications Inc. Gift and matching funds from the National Endowment for the Arts, 1981   1981.1063. Reproduced with permission.
p. 64: *The Figure 5 in Gold*. Alfred Stieglitz Collection, 1949   49.59.1
p. 65: *Becca*. Purchase, Bequest of Miss Adelaide Milton de Groot (1876-1967), by exchange, 1972   1972.127
p. 65: *The Burghers of Calais*. Gift of Iris and B. Gerald Cantor, 1989   1989.407
p. 67: *Matteo Gozzadini* and *Ginevra Lupari*. Robert Lehman Collection, 1975   1975.1.95, 1975.1.96
p. 67: *Two Young Girls at the Piano*. Robert Lehman Collection, 1975   1975.1.201

Photography Credits

Unless otherwise noted, photography is by The Metropolitan Museum of Art Photograph Studio.

Karin L. Willis: p. 5, modern children
Bruce White: p. 5, Petrie Court; p. 6, buttons, Great Hall, maps, Grand Staircase; p. 7, arranging flowers, guard at door, guard directing children; p. 8, dusting vase, climate sensors, climate computer; p. 9, carpentry shop; p. 10, catalogue card; p. 12, curator and designer, designer at board; p. 14, curators discussing, curator researching, curator viewing art; p. 46, piano being played; p. 47, musical instruments conservation; p. 59, costume conservation; p. 61, print study room; p. 66, Lehman gallery
Dan Kershaw: p. 9, riggers uncrating painting; p. 12, exhibition model, gallery model, gallery view; p. 13, building walls, color choices, painting walls, examining art, arranging pictures
Richard Lombard: p. 9, crates on Fifth Avenue, Noguchi supervising installation; p. 13, fitting cases
Schecter Lee: p. 22, Relief of a Winged Deity; p. 38, *Dōmaru*; p. 42, Pair of Ear Spools
Malcolm Varon: p. 34, detail of capital; p. 57, *Cypresses*
Helen Buttfield: p. 37, armor workshop, armor workshop
Haruo Takemoto of the Otsuka Kogesha Co., Ltd.: p. 38, *Wakizashi, Tsuba*
Justin Kerr: p. 44, Horse and Rider
Richard Creek: p. 48, Hart Room
© Nippon Television Network Corporation Tokyo 1991: p. 60, Libyan Sibyl, Sistine Chapel, Vatican

72 Answers

p. 6:   Chinese, Japanese, German, English, French, Spanish, Italian

p. 10: The accession number is 97.34. It indicates that the painting was the 34th object acquired in 1897. From 1870 to 1969, the last two digits of the year were used in the accession number. Since 1970, all four digits are used.

p. 12: The real gallery is on the left.

p. 20: There are 372 pieces of colored stone.

p. 24: It has eight heads.

p. 26: soft, light, smooth, wet, open, curved

p. 32: The spaces between the animal heads are upside-down animal heads.

p. 34: Two lion bodies share a single head.

p. 35: The initials are A and E (the E is reversed).

p. 36: Overlapping plates allow bending at the neck, shoulders, elbows, hands, hips, thighs, knees, and feet.

p. 42: There are at least 85 pieces of shell and stone in each ear spool.

p. 51: 1) The crossing was made in the dark. 2) The horses came later. 3) The ice was thin.

p. 54: Goya's name is on the card in the magpie's beak.

p. 57: The detail is part of the face of the man on the right.

p. 57: A. Seurat, B. Monet, C. Van Gogh

p. 59: The holes are for attaching leggings to the doublet with metal-tipped ribbons called points.

p. 64: "BILL" in the upper left corner; "Carlo" in the upper middle right; and "W.C.W" in the bottom center

Quiz:

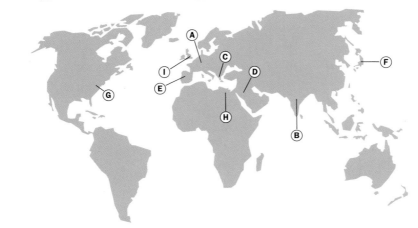

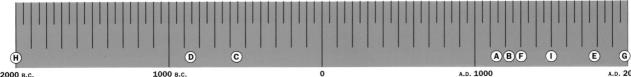

| 2000 B.C. | 1000 B.C. | 0 | A.D. 1000 | A.D. 2000 |

Ask William

The Egyptian hippopotamus that appears on page 21 is the Museum's unofficial mascot, known as William.

Is there anything we haven't told you about the Museum that you'd like to know?
Send your questions to William, and he'll answer them for you.

ASK WILLIAM
c/o Education Department
The Metropolitan Museum of Art
1000 Fifth Avenue
New York, NY 10028
www.metmuseum.org